Academic Writing

Academic Writing

Process and Product

Andrew P. Johnson

ROWMAN & LITTLEFIELD
Lanham • Boulder • New York • London

Published by Rowman & Littlefield
A wholly owned subsidiary of The Rowman & Littlefield Publishing Group, Inc.
4501 Forbes Boulevard, Suite 200, Lanham, Maryland 20706
www.rowman.com

Unit A, Whitacre Mews, 26-34 Stannary Street, London SE11 4AB

British Library Cataloguing in Publication Information Available

Library of Congress Cataloging-in-Publication Data

Names: Johnson, Andrew P. (Andrew Paul) author.
Title: Academic writing : process and product / Andrew P. Johnson.
Description: Lanham, MD : Rowman & Littlefield, [2016] | Includes bibliographical references.
Identifiers: LCCN 2015048754| ISBN 9781475823554 (hardcover : alk. paper) | ISBN 9781475823561 (pbk. : alk. paper) | ISBN 9781475823578 (electronic)
Subjects: LCSH: Academic writing—Study and teaching (Higher) | Critical thinking. | College readers.
Classification: LCC P301.5.A27 J44 2016 | DDC 808/.042—dc23
LC record available at http://lccn.loc.gov/2015048754

∞™ The paper used in this publication meets the minimum requirements of American National Standard for Information Sciences Permanence of Paper for Printed Library Materials, ANSI/NISO Z39.48-1992.

Printed in the United States of America

This book is dedicated to my lovely wife, Dr. Nancy Fitzsimons. She is my rock in tough times and my light in good times.

Contents

Preface

I wrote this book initially because the graduate and undergraduate students in my classes seem to struggle with writing. The common response to poor writing skills at many colleges and universities is to simply require additional writing-intensive courses or to assign more writing in current courses. But these sorts of things by themselves do very little to improve students' ability to write. Why? Because *writing* is a verb. This means a verb sort of instruction is needed.

Too often, academic writing is treated as if it were simply a noun. The focus is on what the product should look like or what the correct word usage should be. These are noun sorts of things, not verb sorts of things. *Writing* is a verb. It is a process. As a matter of fact, it is a complex process. And you learn how to do complex processes best when somebody breaks the complex process down into steps and then describes and demonstrates each step. This is how I taught long division to my second-grade students. This is how I taught single-leg takedowns to my high school wrestlers. This is what I do when I teach college students how to write.

Assigning is different from teaching. Assigning more writing is not an effective way to teach students how to write. Some may figure it out eventually, but many more will be frustrated and learn only how to do enough to pass the course. We cannot expect students to learn to write if we do not teach them how. But we must teach them how, not what. Writing is a how.

This book is about how. You will get to the what only if you first attend to the how.

Introduction

This book provides a foundation and framework to enhance your understanding of the various processes involved in academic writing. The term *academic writing* here refers to the types of writing used in college-level writing courses at both the undergraduate and graduate levels. However, this book was not written simply to help you pass another English class or to get you through the next writing-intensive course (although it will certainly do that). At some point, you will be out in the real world (hopefully); thus, the purpose of this book is to enable you to be an effective writer and thinker in all contexts, including your personal and professional lives (outside a college environment). In this sense, it may be helpful to perceive academic writing in a larger sense as academic and professional writing and thinking.

THE ART, SCIENCE, AND CRAFT OF ACADEMIC WRITING

Academic writing is an art, a science, and a craft.

An Art

It is an art in that your academic writing is ultimately an expression of you and your thinking. Writers are not standardized products with homogenous views and uniform ways of thinking. There is not one specific method or style that works best for all academic writers. There is not a singular best way to approach a topic or question. As an academic writer, you will need to find the strategies that work best for you and develop the writing style that is most effective in conveying your message to your intended audience.

A Science

It is a science in that there are elements of style to which you must adhere as well as specific forms that must be utilized or included. This book contains some of these. You may also wish to refer to the manual within your field. American Psychological Association (APA) style is used in the social sciences, and Modern Language Association (MLA) is used in literature, the arts, and humanities. APA and MLA are the two most common forms required in colleges and universities. Chicago/Turabian is sometimes used in history and other scholarly and nonscholarly works. American Medical Association (AMA) style is used in medicine, health, and other biological sciences.

A Craft

Academic writing can also be described as a craft. A craft is a skill or set of skills developed over time through experience. This is exactly what writing of any kind is. You cannot expect to master this particular form of writing after taking one course or reading one book. Good writers learn their craft and develop their writing abilities over time. It takes practice, experience, reflection, and a desire to improve.

IT IS ALL ABOUT THE PROCESS

There are three big ideas to carry with you as you begin: First, this book describes a process. A process is a systematic series of actions or steps designed to achieve a particular end. In this case, the designated end is a well-written piece of academic writing. The written product is a result of the process. Understanding the process involved is the most important element in becoming an effective academic writer.

Second, this book will not teach you how to write. You already know how to do this. You know how to put words on the page to create and express ideas. It may be that you are not a very good writer or that you do not understand academic writing (this can be easily fixed), but you can write. The way to become an effective academic writer is to embrace the process (see earlier). However, this process will be building on that which you already know how to do.

Third, academic writing is not difficult or complicated—*if you attend to the process*. So let us begin.

I

The Process of Academic Writing

Chapter One

The Super-Secret Academic Writing Process Revealed

Academic writing is not an event but a process that occurs over time.

Academic writing is easy as long as you understand and trust the process. This chapter starts with an overview of academic writing and ends with a description of the super-secret process used for academic writing.

THE BIG PICTURE

Academic writing is different in form and function from creative writing. Its basic purpose is to present information or transmit ideas as efficiently and economically as possible. Academic writing is used to write academic reports, inquiries (research), and essays in academic settings. A variation of this form is also valued in most business and professional settings.

Creative writing is used to tell a story or to evoke an emotional or aesthetic response. Its purpose is to entertain or inspire. Here, the writer is able to inject his or her insights and emotion all over the page and use words and language like colors on a pallet to paint a picture. Academic writing is not like that. It is more formal, uses structure to carry ideas, seldom contains dialogue, and is purposefully objective. Good academic writers take themselves out of the paper to the greatest extent possible and let ideas and data carry their paper. Note the following differences:

1. *Creative writing.* As I walked slowly into the dungy gymnasium, I couldn't believe my eyes. The gym was packed with wild and crazy students all shouting their lungs out, cheering on their beloved basket-

ball team. The crazed team seemed to absorb their energy and was playing with grit and determination, giving everything they had to beat the hated visiting rival from Shelbyville.

2. *Academic writing.* The home basketball team played Shelbyville in front of a large crowd of enthusiastic fans.

TYPES OF ACADEMIC WRITING

There are three common types of academic writing:

1. *Expository writing.* The purpose of this type of writing is to explain, describe, provide information, or communicate knowledge in some form.
2. *Persuasive writing.* The purpose of this type of writing is to make a case for or against an issue using concise, objective language and sound reasoning.
3. *Inquiry writing.* Inquiry is the process of asking a question, gathering data, and then using that data to answer the question. *Inquiry* is another name for *research*. Data can be gathered using primary sources through direct observation, survey, interviews, or other means. Data can also be collected using such secondary sources as peer-reviewed research and scholarly articles and books. The purpose of this type of writing is to describe all phases of the inquiry process.

THE ACADEMIC WRITING PROCESS

Academic writing is not an event that occurs in one setting but a process that occurs over time. This process is necessarily messy. In the process of academic writing, you will need to think, plan, struggle, revise, rewrite, and mess about in order to discover exactly what it is you want to say and how you want to say it. This is all part of the process (see Textbox 1.1). Each step of this process is revealed in this chapter. Chapters 2 through 5 describe and demonstrate each of these steps in the academic writing process.

The Academic Writing Process

1. *Research to gather data.* Usually this means finding sources, reading, and taking careful notes. However, data can also be collected other ways.

2. *Predraft.* As the name implies, this is what is done before writing the first draft. This involves such things as planning, creating outlines, talking with others, generating ideas, or finding structure.
3. *Write a first draft (sloppy copy).* This is the first attempt to get ideas on the page.
4. *Revise.* This is the heart of the writing process. Here, the writer rereads, reshapes, gets feedback, and revises many times.
5. *Edit.* Editing should occur only after a piece has been revised several times. Here, the writer looks for spelling, punctuation, and grammatical errors.
6. *Share or publish.* This is the very last step. This is where the paper is sent out into the world.

Step 1: Research to Gather Data

You cannot write unless you have something to write about. Thus, the first step in the academic writing process is to research to gather data. This is usually done by reading critically and taking careful notes (see Chapter 2). Data can also be collected through interviews, observations, inquiries, or surveys. This will provide the information necessary to write. In academic writing, having a cohesive body of information in front of you makes the process much easier and greatly enhances the quality of your final product. Skipping or minimizing your effort here makes writing much more difficult in all subsequent phases.

Step 2: Predraft

Once you have gathered data and taken notes, the next step is to generate ideas and find a basic yet flexible initial structure. Following are five strategies for this. Note that there is no single strategy that is best for every person or every writing situation. Find the one that works best for you. Adopt and adapt. Again, your initial structure should come from your data. Thus, reading widely and taking careful notes is a crucial first step. You cannot get to Step 2 without fully engaging in Step 1.

Brainstorm and List

Use a yellow legal pad or sheet of notepaper, and start listing ideas as quickly as you can. After you have a paper filled with scratches and messy sentences, look for patterns and groups. Use these to create a very flexible, beginning structure or an initial outline.

Brainstorm and Group

First, write your topic at the top of a sheet of paper. Then generate and list as many ideas as quickly as you can that are related to your topic without regard to evaluation. That is, whenever you brainstorm, you should include the silly, far-fetched ideas along with the more pragmatic ones. Ideas that may be considered conceptual outliers serve to stretch the boundaries of your think- ing and enable you to think more broadly about your topic. Use single words or short abbreviated phrases to hold each idea. Next, look for groups or patterns. Finally, organize the ideas into groups to create sections and para- graphs.

Semantic Webs

The semantic web allows you to generate ideas at the same time as you create structure. It tends to create a more visual structure. First, draw a circle in the middle of your paper and write your topic in the circle. Then, identify three or four ideas related to your topic. Each of these becomes a node (see Figure 1.1). Next, identify important ideas for each node. Finally, use this flexible structure to begin writing. Each node of your web will become sections or paragraphs.

Talking

Talking through your writing project or explaining it to a friend or colleague helps to organize the ideas in your head and detect any missing parts. En- courage friends and colleagues to ask questions or add ideas as you explain your topic.

Power Writing

Power writing helps you get in touch with your unconscious. Set a timer for three minutes. Starting with your writing topic, write as many things as quickly as you can for one to three minutes. Do not overthink here. The goal is to create an abundance of ideas, both good and bad. Do not let your pen stop moving. Use free association to catch the first thing that pops into your mind. Let your mind travel. It does not matter if you jump from one idea to the next or if your ideas are jumbled. You will get it straightened out later.

Step 3: Write a First Draft (Sloppy Copy)

The first draft is your initial attempt to get ideas on paper. The first draft becomes an external version of your working memory used to hold all your thoughts and ideas as you generate and organize them and as you look for associations and supporting ideas. The first draft should be a poorly written,

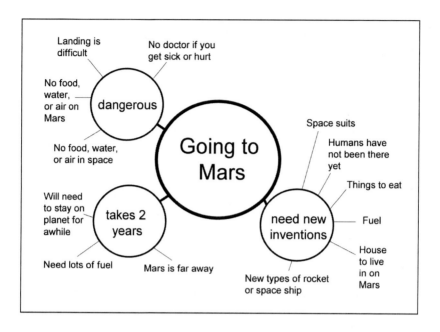

Figure 1.1. Semantic web.

unorganized pile of garbage. Only then can you start to pull things away and begin to see some of the good ideas emerging. You have to throw that first blob of clay on the potter's wheel before you begin shaping it.

You must get your initial ideas on the page without evaluating them. Strive for quantity versus quality at this stage. Celebrate really bad writing. It is the first step toward really good writing.

Step 4: Revise

Revision (re-vision) means "to see again" or, in this case, "to see again and again and again." Revision is at the heart of the super-secret academic writing process. As described previously, the first draft is like a potter throwing the first glob of clay on the wheel. Revision is where the potter begins to shape the clay. And remember, a potter does not spin the wheel once or twice and consider the pot to be finished. There is always a great deal of shaping and reshaping. New clay is added; some is taken away.

The same applies to academic writing. Expect to revise your academic writing a minimum of 4 times but usually 10 to 15 times. In the revision step, you should not worry about spelling and punctuation; rather, try to find a logical organization, and listen to see if your sentences and paragraphs make sense. You will be editing in Step 5.

Step 5: Edit

Editing is the fifth step. Here, you run your writing through a spell-check program and concentrate on correct grammar, punctuation, word usage, and citations. Everybody needs an editor. Thus, it is helpful at this stage to have others read your work to look for errors in grammar, punctuation, and word choice and also to provide feedback. The feedback you get from others will give you a sense of how the ideas are playing inside the readers' heads. This feedback also enables you to identify those parts of your paper that may be unclear or confusing. Step 5 may send you back to an earlier step. Very rarely will you move through the steps in an orderly, linear fashion. It is common to repeat some steps several times.

Step 6: Share or Publish

The last step is to share your writing with the world.

HOW TO AVOID WRITER'S BLOCK

Sometimes when attempting to write, words and ideas just do not come out. This is commonly known as writer's block. This often means that you are trying to get it just right the first time. That is, you are trying to generate ideas and evaluate ideas at the same time. Do not do this.

Writing involves two opposite mental operations: generating and evaluating. Your brain needs to generate in order to get an abundance of words and ideas with which to write, but it also needs to evaluate in order to throw out some of the words and ideas and to reshape or revise others. Your brain does both of these mental operations rather well but not at the same time.

If you find yourself in a state of writer's block, do not panic. Getting stuck is common. Chapter 4 describes some ideas to get you unstuck and to get the words and ideas flowing again.

LAST WORD

Academic writing is easy; however, this does not mean that it is quick.

Chapter Two

Research to Gather Data

Academic writing is easy if you follow the steps. It is difficult if you do not.

Academic writing involves saying something about something. Thus, you need information to convey, analyze, or use in some fashion. As stated in the last chapter, finding new information and taking careful notes is the first step of the academic writing process. You cannot get to Step 2 without doing Step 1.

> *Step 1: Research to gather data.* Usually this means reading and taking careful notes. However, data can also be collected other ways.

In the typical academic writing scenario, you have or are given a topic, question, idea, or position about which you need to write, define, explain, or defend. Okay, then what?

FIND AND USE CREDIBLE SOURCES

First, you need to find some credible sources of information to use. You most likely are not a credible source. Thus, your academic writing will have no credibility unless you find and use credible sources. Credible sources in academic writing include the following.

Academic Journals

Academic journals are the best sources to use for academic writing. These contain articles written by specialists in various fields. Academic journals describe research, secondary research, novel applications of existing theories, or new or interesting ideas set in a theoretical context. There are hundreds of different academic journals in all areas, from medicine to psychology, accounting, religion, and even humor (*International Journal of Humor Research*).

An academic journal is not the same as a magazine. Magazines are designed to attract a wide audience and make a profit for the publisher. They are usually written by a staff of writers or reporters who do not have special expertise in the fields about which they are reporting. Also, magazines depend on advertising revenue. This affects the kinds of things that are published. Thus, even if something is published in a very prominent, nationally known magazine (or website), it cannot be considered a credible source.

Academic journals are designed to inform the field. They do not employ a staff of writers. Instead, scientists, researchers, teachers, and other professionals in various fields send in their work to be considered for publication. Each article is peer reviewed, which means it is critiqued by a jury of three to six experts in the field to check for accuracy and validity. Each reviewer then makes a recommendation about whether to accept the article for publication. Often, many revisions are made before an article is finally accepted for publication.

Books

Books can be credible sources; however, just because it is written in a book does not make it true. Books published by major publishing houses can generally be trusted to provide credible information if they cite their sources. However, you always need to look at the references at the end of a book to evaluate the sources. In most fields, articles found in respected, peer-reviewed academic journals are still the gold standard. This is what most look for when evaluating the credibility of a book.

Reports, Position Papers, Monographs, and Other Documents

Besides academic books and articles published in academic journals, there are other types of documents that can be considered credible sources for academic writing. These can include reports, position papers, monographs, or articles published by reputable institutions such as a respected university, a well-known nongovernment organization, or even a government program or department. For example, in the area of literacy, any report, position paper, monograph, or article put out by the International Literacy Association (ILA;http://www.literacyworldwide.org/) or the National Council of Teachers of English (NCTE: http://www.ncte.org/) could be considered to be a credible source. These are academic organizations consisting of thousands of teachers, researchers, scholars, parents, writers, publishers, and other professionals in areas related to literacy. In the same way, there are reports and other types information put out by the Government Accounting Office (GAO: http://www.gao.gov/), the National Assessment of Educational Progress (NAEP: https://nces.ed.gov/nationsreportcard/), and other government agencies that would be considered to be nonbiased and credible.

When looking at these types of documents, there are no hard and fast rules about what is and is not credible. However, here are three simple tips to help you analyze and evaluate these sources: First, look at the reference list. Check to see if the sources cited are from reputable peer-reviewed journals and academic book publishers. Second, check for possible bias or conflicts of interest with the organization's goals or mission. Third, check to see if the author has training, background knowledge, or expertise in the area in which he or she is writing. For example, a reading researcher or literacy scholar writing about reading instruction would tend to be more credible than, say, a physicist or psychologist.

One rule of thumb: Never rely on a single source or a single type of source in your academic writing. In order to get a clear and accurate picture of anything, use multiple sources (the more the better), multiple types of sources, and multiple perspectives. This is why program developers, curriculum planners, researchers, and academic writers include a review of the literature (all the literature) in their work and not simply a review of a single article or study.

GATHER DATA USING CREDIBLE SOURCES

It is common to spend considerable time during the beginning stages of your writing project looking for sources, reading critically, and taking notes. However, spending a little extra time up front saves you a great deal of time and frustration later on. The substeps are listed here.

Step 1A: Start With a Clearly Defined Writing Topic or Question

This will enhance your efficiency as you look for sources. However, be flexible. Remember, you are not a knowledgeable expert at this stage. Often your initial writing topic or question will change slightly in the beginning stages based on the data you gather. Also, keep your topic or question as simple as possible. This will enable you to effectively understand the basic dimensions of your topic.

Step 1B: Locate Possible Sources Related to Your Writing Topic or Question

For academic writing, you will need to look for sources in a college library or on the Internet. Most public libraries do not have the academic journals or other sources that you will need.

Step 1C: Peruse Your Sources

Once you have located all your sources, make sure they contain information related to your question. For books, check the table of contents and the index and then scan a few chapters. For journal articles, read the abstract and scan the headings, subheadings, and final paragraph. Spending a few minutes here will save you a great deal of time later on.

Step 1D: Read Critically and Take Careful Notes

This substep is so important that it has its own subsection.

READ CRITICALLY AND TAKE CAREFUL NOTES

Read Critically

Reading critically means that you make decisions about what is important (and not) as you are reading. In your notes, do not attempt to remember or replicate the complete chapter or article. Instead, select and record only that information that is relevant to your writing topic or question, hence the importance of Step 1A.

Take Careful Notes

Sometimes beginning academic writers think they can save time by skipping note-taking. They try to read their material and just highlight the salient points with a highlighter. This does not work. Not only do these writers end up spending a great deal more time on their writing projects, but also the writing derived from this approach tends to be vague and ill-defined, lacks structure and substance, and is incoherent.

Begin your note-taking by writing the full reference citation at the top of the page (see Textbox 2.1). Having this here will save you the task of having to look up the articles again when creating the reference list (see Chapter 19). Next, use a very basic outline form, recording only those ideas needed to support your writing topic. Use short, concise, incomplete sentences with just enough words to hold the idea. The goal during note-taking is not to create grammatically correct writing; rather, it is to restate and remember the authors' ideas in a way that makes them readily accessible to you. Use 10-point font, single spacing, with half-inch margins to maximize the information visible on a single page. Finally, record your notes using only one side of the page. This allows you to spread all your notes out in front of you when you begin to write your first draft so that you can more easily identify common themes or patterns.

Example of Notes for an Academic Article
Notes for Vocabulary

Ebbers, S. M., & Denton, C. A. (2008). A root awakening: Vocabulary instruction for older students with reading difficulties. *Learning Disabilities Research and Practice, 23,* 90–102.

1. Learning reading skills: best word learning strategies
   a. teach reading skills improve vocab
2. Takes several encounters to learn new word (6–7)
   a. students with RD need more reps
3. Struggling readers tend to avoid reading—resulting in less vocab growth
4. Students RD often have trouble inferring meanings of new words
5. Principles of effective vocab instruct
   a. explicit instruction
   b. teach students to apply cog and metacog. strategies
   c. use questioning approaches including self-questioning to promote active cognitive interaction with text.
   d. promote collaborative engagements in learning with opps. for students to talk.
   e. provide opp's for students to practice.

AN EXAMPLE OF THE PROCESS

You will be successful with your academic writing if you understand and implement the process. The following example may help to make this process more salient.

Finding Credible Sources

Sally was writing a paper on vocabulary instruction. She went to her university library to get eight books that she had identified as being relevant. While looking for these books, she found two additional titles on the shelves that she had not considered. She brought all of these to a table, where she quickly scanned the tables of contents, reference lists, and individual chapters to see if there were relevant data. Of these ten books, she found that only six were helpful. She was able to discard four. Spending a little time here saved her a lot of time later on. Also, she only had to check out and lug around six books instead of ten. These books were taken home for critical reading and note-taking (see earlier).

A similar processed was used to find academic journal articles. After identifying a list of nine articles, she was able to find seven of these (her university had a subscription service to many academic journals). Just like the books, she skimmed the abstracts as well as the conclusions and last sections of each. All of these contained relevant data. Thus, she downloaded and printed all of them.

Reading and Note-Taking

Each person has a process that works best for him or her for critical reading and note-taking. A process that many have found to be effective is described here.

First, make sure your topic or question is clearly identified. This creates focus for your reading and will help you to see the important ideas. Second, look at the headings and read the final paragraph to get an overview of the chapter or article. This enhances comprehension because you have a sense of structure and you can see how one thing connects to another. Third, read the article quickly, putting a dot or dash in the margin next to the ideas you feel to be important. Do not take notes during your initial read because it interrupts the flow of comprehension. Fourth, after you have finished reading, go back and highlight those ideas that were marked. This serves two purposes: (a) It reinforces salient ideas, and (b) it makes rereading and seeing these ideas easier. Finally, record the ideas on paper or a computer. If what you are reading is unfamiliar or overly complex, then it is helpful to take notes using paper and then retype them into the computer. The process of writing, retyping, analyzing, and finding important ideas invites you to process the information at deeper levels and helps with comprehension.

This is one process that many use. Adopt and adapt, or find your own process. The point is this: You cannot expect to take shortcuts at this stage. Trying to take shortcuts during this step will increase the amount of time spent on your paper, escalate the level of frustration and anxiety, and reduce the quality of your final written product.

Two Tricks for Finding Sources

Here are two simple tricks for finding sources: First, when you encounter a book or article that is particularly helpful, see what sources are being cited and look these up. Each source usually can lead to additional sources. And when you see the same sources cited in a variety of books and articles, you begin to get a sense of what the experts in the field consider relevant. It does not take too long before you have a good sense of the topic.

Second, articles cited in books and journals can often be found on the Internet. For example, during Sally's review of the literature, she came across the reference in Textbox 2.2. She copied the complete citation and pasted it in her Internet search engine. She was able to find a complete copy of this article on a website called *LD Online*. While this technique does not always lead to a copy of the complete article, you will often find that it may lead you to other good academic journal articles.

Example of a Reference

Lane, H. B., & Allen, S. A. (2010). The vocabulary-rich classroom: Modeling sophisticated word use to promote word consciousness and vocabulary growth. *The Reading Teacher, 63,* 362–370. http://www.ldonline.org/article/40991/

THE NEXT STEP

Once you have carefully read your articles and taken notes, the next step is to package the ideas so that they can be easily understood by your reader. This means putting the ideas into groups or categories and finding structure. This is described in the next chapter.

Chapter Three

Predraft

Structure is the basis of all things.

Step 2: Predraft. As the name implies, this is what is done before writing the first draft. This involves such things as planning, creating outlines, talking with others, generating ideas, or finding structure.

FINDING A BEGINNING STRUCTURE

Identifying an initial structure to use for your paper will enable you to be much more effective and efficient in your academic writing. It will also result in a more readable final product. (Structure enhances comprehension.) The initial structure you create should arise from the data (your notes). The term *initial structure* is used here because it is common for this structure to evolve as you encounter more data. The following is one process that can be used to find structure. As always, adopt and adapt.

1. Print Notes

As stated in the last chapter, your notes should be single-spaced and single-sided. Make sure you can clearly see the titles, headings, and subheadings. Print out your notes, and spread them out in front of you.

2. Look for Groups

Look for common ideas, similar concepts, or related themes (groups). Use some method to identify these initial groups in your notes. Some prefer to use a colored highlighter here. You could also use a simple label written in the margin. Again, these initial groups are all flexible. As you encounter new data and reread and review your notes, these initial groups will evolve.

For example, when reviewing her notes on vocabulary instruction, Sally saw the following five general themes emerge: (a) how children learn new words, (b) the importance of word knowledge, (c) reading and vocabulary, (d) teaching strategies to enhance vocabulary, and (e) graphic organizers. These eventually morphed into the four general groups, or categories, in Textbox 3.1.

Groups Arising From Notes

1. Attending to vocabulary
2. General principles for developing students' vocabulary
3. Strategies for developing students' vocabulary
4. Visual displays and graphic organizers

* The groups above would eventually be used for headings.

---

3. Create Headings and Move Ideas

Create an initial heading for each of your groups. Then use the cut-and-paste function to begin moving your ideas from your notes into groups.

4. Identify Ideas

As you move an idea into a group, use some system to identify where the idea came from. This will enable you to cite it later on. For example: In writing her paper on vocabulary instruction, Sally wanted to use an idea from an article by Lane and Allen (2010; see Textbox 3.2). She first moved this idea into the correct group. Then, to remember where she got the idea, she used "LA10" as a designator. This refers to Lane and Allen (2010).

Example of Note-Taking

Lane, H. B., & Allen, S. A. (2010). The vocabulary-rich classroom: Modeling sophisticated word use to promote word consciousness and vocabulary growth. *The Reading Teacher, 63,* 362–370.

1. Vocab—Pre/K—one of best predictors of later reading comp, reading performance, school achievement (LA10).

5. Consolidate Ideas

Look for similar ideas within each group. Consolidate these while keeping the designator. For example, Sally noticed an idea similar to that in Textbox 3.2 in an article by Stahl (1999). She listed this under the same category heading. When it came time to consolidate her notes under each heading, she incorporated them into a single sentence and included the designator 'S99' so that she could cite this correctly later on (See Textbox 3.3).

Consolidating Ideas in Your Notes

1. Vocab—Pre/K—one of best predictors of later reading comp, reading performance, school achievement (LA10, S99).

6. Cross Off Ideas Used

As Sally put each idea into a group, she used a highlighter to cross it off the notes she had printed out. Once all her ideas were in groups, she was then ready to begin constructing an extremely rough first draft (see Chapter 4).

BUT WAIT—

The process described here may not work for you. You will need to have options. You can also use any of the five predrafting strategies described in Chapter 1. Two additional strategies are described here.

List and Group

There are times when you have too much information and you do not know how to put structure to it. The "List and Group" strategy can be helpful in these instances. Here, you simply start listing salient, interesting, or important ideas on a blank sheet of paper. Do this apart from your notes initially. Do not worry about structure or organization; rather, just get ideas on the page without evaluating. As the ideas appear on the page, you will begin to see structure emerging. Create an initial outline from this. Next, review your notes. Use these to inform or revise your structure. Finally, move to the computer, insert your group headings, and begin listing ideas from your notes under your headings (see earlier).

Free Write

Sometimes the structure you need is gurgling in your unconscious, but your conscious mind gets in the way. A strategy to use here is called the "Free Write." Here, you turn away from your notes and use a blank sheet of paper to write as quickly as you can. Resist the temptation to edit yourself in any way. You are trying to create a pile of gravel. From this pile of gravel, you will begin to see some precious nuggets and structure emerge. This is different from the power write strategy described in Chapter 1 in that there is no time limit here.

THE LAST WORD ABOUT SHORTCUTS

Reading critically, taking notes, and finding structure are important parts of the academic writing process. Shortcuts taken at this stage always end up being long cuts. Take the time to read critically, take careful notes, and find an initial structure from which to write. It will save you time and result in a much better written product.

REFERENCES

Lane, H. B., & Allen, S. A. (2010). The vocabulary-rich classroom: Modeling sophisticated word use to promote word consciousness and vocabulary growth. *The Reading Teacher, 63,* 362–370.
Stahl, S. (1999). *Vocabulary development.* Brookline, MA: Brookline Books.

Chapter Four

Draft and Revise

You cannot create high-quality writing if you are not first willing to create garbage. If you look underneath a cow pie, you will find lots of green stuff growing.

Step 3: Write a first draft (sloppy copy). This is the first attempt to get ideas on the page.

Step 4: Revise. This is the heart of the writing process. Here the writer rereads, reshapes, gets feedback, and revises many times.

AN EXTREMELY ROUGH FIRST DRAFT

The last chapter describes how to organize the ideas from your notes into groups. These groups will provide a flexible structure to use to begin writing your extremely rough first draft. Once you have your ideas in groups, you are ready for Step 3: the first draft.

Making a Clay Pot

As described in Chapter 1, writing is like making a clay pot. A potter takes a big glob of clay and throws it on a spinning wheel. The potter then spends a great deal of time shaping and molding the pot before finally putting it into the furnace to bake. However, without first putting that big blob of clay on the wheel, there would be no pot.

The first draft is your big glob of clay. When you write, you have to start with a big glob of ideas. A first draft is your initial attempt to get these ideas on the page. This should be done without regard to the final product.

For example, when Sally wrote the first draft of her paper on vocabulary instruction, she threw all sorts of stuff on the page. She had an outline to give her a general sense of where she was going, but at this stage, she was just throwing ideas on the page. She knew that she would have to go back many times to reread, revise, reshape, review, remove, and restate.

Embracing Contraries

Writing involves two separate and diametrically opposed cognitive processes: generating ideas and evaluating ideas (Elbow, 1998). As a writer, you need to put things on the page, and you need to take things off. Both types of thinking are necessary during the writing process. But if you try to do both at the same time, then you will clog up the writing mechanism.

You cannot write well if you are not first willing to write poorly. Thus, when you start your academic paper, your goal should be to write garbage. You should strive to create a terrible paper. This will free you up to get your ideas on the page. During the revision process, you will be moving your ideas around and throwing away much of what you write anyway; thus, it makes little sense to try to get a polished product at this stage. There will be time enough to polish and revise during Step 4, revising, and Step 5, editing.

Some prefer to have their first drafts handwritten. The handwritten first draft allows you to quickly scratch things out, use arrows, and even insert diagrams in the margins. Keep in mind that there is no single writing strategy that works best for all people all the time. Find that strategy that work best for you.

Connecting

As you begin to throw ideas on the page during the first draft, you often discover a couple of really good ideas that you had not considered previously. Quickly throwing ideas on the page frees up your unconscious mind to make all sorts of connections and associations. You will find that there are lots of good ideas laying around your unconscious mind ready to be used.

REVISING: MAKING MANY VISITS

Revising (Step 4) is at the heart of the academic writing process. When you revise, you review (see again) and revisit a piece. During the revision process, you will need to make many visits back to your writing.

Whole to Part to Whole

Revising works best when you go from whole to part to whole. That means you must have a poorly written first draft (whole) to begin the revision process. Here is how you do it:

1. Start the revision process with the first sentence. Focus only on this sentence. Make sure that sentence makes sense and that you use as few words as possible. Good academic writing uses as few words as possible (see Chapter 8). Take any words out that do not absolutely need to be there.

2. When that sentence is as concise and coherent as possible, go to the next sentence. Then, go to the next. Repeat the process with all the sentences in the paragraph.

3. Now, focus on that paragraph. Make sure the paragraph (a) says exactly what you want it to say, (b) does not repeat any ideas, and (c) uses as few words as possible. Reread this paragraph many times. Sometimes it is helpful to read the paragraph out loud to develop a writer's ear. Do not move to the next paragraph until the current paragraph meets these three conditions.

4. Then move to the next paragraph. Repeat the process starting with the first sentence.

5. When you have completed all the paragraphs in a section of your paper, reread, review, and revise just that section. Remove any paragraphs, ideas, sentences, or words that do not absolutely need to be there. Make sure each paragraph flows smoothly from one to the next (transition words and sentences are described in Chapter 13). When that section is just as you want it, it should read like melted butter. Then go to the next section. Repeat the process starting with the first sentence.

6. When you have done this with each sentence, paragraph, and section, do this with the complete paper.

Melted Butter

Good academic writing reads like melted butter. It flows off the page. You cannot help but understand what the writer is trying to say. You do not have to pause or reread to figure out awkward sentences or sudden shifts in subject. Melted butter should always be the goal of revising.

There is nothing overly complicated about this butter-making process. Just follow the steps. Sit down in the chair, take a deep breath, and do it. Academic writing is easy if you relax and use the process.

YOUR UNCONSCIOUS MIND IS YOUR FRIEND

In the middle of writing her paper on vocabulary instruction, Sally discovered that she had much that she wanted to say, but the words seemed to splatter all over the page in random fashion. Nothing was connected. When she read back what she had written, she hated it. This is very common with academic writing. When it happens to you, don't panic.

The problem for Sally was that she was thinking too much. This excess logical thought made it very hard for her conscious mind to access the wealth of ideas bubbling in her unconscious. She needed to find a way to connect with her unconscious mind.

Free Write

The free write, as discussed briefly in Chapter 3, is an effective strategy to use here. Sally grabbed a pencil and legal pad, pulled out her notes, found an interesting idea to use to prime the pump, and just started writing. She wrote down the first thing that popped into her mind related to her writing topic. The ideas that began to appear on the page were strange and disjoined at first; however, as she continued to write, she started to get a sense of where she wanted to go with the paper. And the more she wrote, the more the ideas seemed to flow onto the page. In about seven minutes, she had three pages of scribbled words, sentences, half sentences, and even diagrams. Much of what she wrote was garbage; however, in that pile of garbage, she found three very good ideas that she had not previously considered. Also, out of her pile of garbage, she began to see a structure for her paper that she had not previously considered. Her conscious mind could now see how the parts might be put together to create a logical whole.

Your unconscious mind is your friend. Undisturbed by conscious contamination, ideas grow here like bacteria in a petri dish. The free write is one way to access the ideas in your unconscious mind. Following are three other techniques that can be used.

Take a Nap

It is difficult for most people to operate at peak mental efficiency for 8 to 10 hours straight. Often, a 10- to 15-minute power nap is all it takes to enable your conscious mind to become more refreshed and revitalized in the process. And it allows your unconscious mind to burp up ideas that are lingering there.

Do Something Else

Leave your writing for a day and then come back. While you are off doing other things, your unconscious mind is still hard at work. This is one of the many reasons you should always start your writing projects well ahead of the deadline. You need to have time and space for some good unconscious percolating.

Think About Nothing

A good way to think about something is to think about nothing. To do this, find a quiet place where you can sit, relax, and get comfortable. Next, close your eyes, and begin to take long, slow, rhythmic breaths. With each breath, picture the air coming in through your nose, filling your body, and then leaving. Finally, empty your mind by thinking of a nonsense word, such as *abba-dabba*, or *in-out*. Repeat this phrase with every inhalation and exhalation. Nature abhors a vacuum, and the vacuum you create will quickly be filled with ideas.

ANOTHER WRITING TRICK: THE BONE PILE

When trying to communicate a coherent message, having too many words can be just as damaging as having too few words. When revising, having too many words on the page can impede the flow of ideas. However, it is often difficult to throw things away once you have worked so hard to write them. A psychological trick to use in this situation is called the bone pile. Here you cut out those things that you think you can do without and move them down to the very bottom of the page in a section called the "bone pile." This is a pile of discarded sentences and paragraphs. This gets them out of the way so you can see what you are working with; however, you know that you can still go back and retrieve them if necessary. This makes them much easier to pull out. Included here is a sample bone pile for this chapter. This bone pile is a garbage dump for old discarded ideas, and thus, it should make little sense to you.

BONE PILE

- Again, the goal is to splash it on the page and keep moving on. You will come back to shape it later.
- Words that do not exactly fit are more apt to cause your message not to be read or understood.

- But, I did go back and research the writing manuals, as well as my own class notes to see what information I needed to convey about developing a sense of audience.
- If that's your goal . . .
- When you revise, you revisit a piece. When you review, you view it again. During revision, you will make many visits back to your writing and view it many times.
- Beginning academic writers often do not have a good sense of how their words should sound. With a great deal of writing practice, you will eventually develop a writer's ear for the sound of the written language.
- Listening to your own writing this way will always result in clarification for you.
- Your notes are the fuel that powers the great writing.
- There are very few first-drafters in the world. These are writers who get it just right the first time.
- However, knowing that I can come back and use discarded ideas makes it much easier to get them out.

WRITER'S BLOCK

It is a common phenomenon. You have a paper, article, or chapter to write. You sit down, and suddenly, you have no idea what to write. Everything that appears on the page is mush. Nothing makes sense. You start to panic. The more you panic, the harder it becomes to write. You tell yourself you are a failure. You will never pass the course, finish the thesis, or get published. What do you do?

First step: Don't panic. All writers experience this. The following are four simple strategies to use here.

1. Read and Take Notes

Reading is like refueling. It provides fuel for your writing machine. Usually, if you do not know what to say, then it is because you do not have enough to say. The only way to have more to say in academic writing is to get more data. Either reread some of your earlier sources or look for more sources.

2. Go Back to the Beginning and Start Revising and Editing

Calm your mind. Going back to the beginning and revising and editing gives you a sense of the whole. You will find parts that can be included and changed. A common cause of writer's block is that you do not have a sense of the whole.

3. Make a List

Using a pencil and legal pad, list those ideas you want to express. Seeing just the list enables you to get a sense of how one thing connects to another. You can get an enhanced sense of structure or see new connecting and supporting ideas.

4. Use Predrafting Strategies

If you get stuck, then use any of the predrafting ideas or activities described in Chapters 1 and 2 at any point in your paper to get unstuck.

THE LAST WORD

As stated previously, revising is at the heart of the academic writing process. Effective academic writers are simply ineffective academic writers who revise a lot.

REFERENCE

Elbow, P. (1998). *Writing without teachers* (2nd ed.). New York: Oxford University Press.

Chapter Five

Edit and Share

We are not good or bad writers; rather, we are writers with the potential for good and bad writing within us.

Step 5: Edit. Editing should occur only after a piece has been revised several times. Here, the writer looks for spelling, punctuation, and grammatical errors.

Step 6: Share or publish. This is the very last step. This is where the paper is sent out into the world.

EDITING

This chapter describes the last two steps of the academic writing process. Step 5 is to edit your piece. If you have not done so, then run your piece through a spell check and grammar check. Also, print your paper and go through it line by line. You will see things on a paper copy that you do not see on a computer screen. Finally, it is very important that you have somebody else read your paper. Because you are so close to your paper, you will often not see simple errors. Also, having somebody else read it will give you a good sense of what elements are confusing. Find somebody you trust here. Have them write their comments directly on your paper. Ask them to identify those things that do not make sense or are worded in ways that are confusing.

Writing Groups

Writing groups are an effective way to get feedback on your work and improve your writing skills. They are used most effectively during the editing phase. Here, people meet in groups of two to eight to read and respond to each other's writing. You can form these groups as part of any class that involves writing. You can also create writing groups on your own apart from any class structure. There are two basic ways to conduct writing groups: first reads and deep reads. Each is described here.

First Read

Here, you read a person's paper for the first time when you meet in the writing group. This is a quick and easy way to get feedback, and it does not require any preparation. Each person brings one copy of his or her edited paper to the group. Trade papers with another member of the group. Each group member responds by writing directly on the copy. When finished, the paper is passed along to another person. In each session, you should get at least four people to respond to each paper.

When you get your paper back, you have the thoughts of different people written at specific places on it. The paper feels alive. You have a sense of how this paper plays inside the heads of different readers. Figure 5.1 contains ideas that can be used as a guide for responding to papers in writing groups.

Figure 5.1　　Ideas for Responding to Papers in Writing Groups

1. What do you like?
2. What questions do you have?
3. What do you want to know more about?
4. What doesn't make sense or gets confusing?
5. What could be added or included?
6. Other comments:

During this process, you might also get help with editing. Remember, you have been living with your writing topic for a while. You are not able to see it as objectively as somebody reading the paper for the first time.

Deep Read

For a deep read, make a copy of your paper for each member of the group. Members should be given a copy a minimum of two days before the writing group meets (one week is best). To be effective, each member of the group must come to the writing group prepared. Feedback is given on each paper in the form of written comments *before* the group meets.

During the writing group session, 10 to 15 minutes is spent on each member's paper. Each group member should describe what they perceive to be the strengths of the paper but also suggest possible changes that can be made. Getting feedback is an important part of the writing process. Giving and receiving honest feedback is the best way to improve as a writer. The rating checklist in Figure 5.2 can be used to help with this process.

Make sure you have defined time limits for each person's paper before beginning the session. Set a timer so that all papers get equal time and attention.

SHARING

The final step in the academic writing process is to let your paper loose into the world. Here you turn it in, send it out, or post it someplace for all to see. The only thing to say in regards to this is that once you let your paper loose,

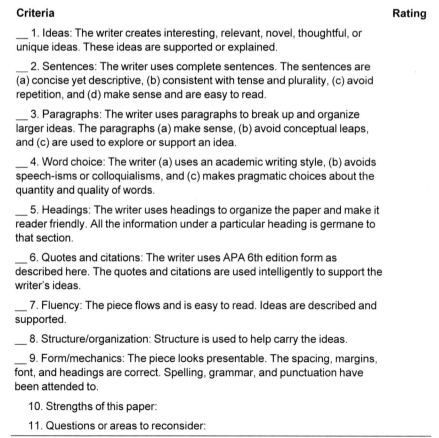

Figure 5.2   Rating Checklist for Academic Writing

Criteria   **Rating**

__ 1. Ideas: The writer creates interesting, relevant, novel, thoughtful, or unique ideas. These ideas are supported or explained.

__ 2. Sentences: The writer uses complete sentences. The sentences are (a) concise yet descriptive, (b) consistent with tense and plurality, (c) avoid repetition, and (d) make sense and are easy to read.

__ 3. Paragraphs: The writer uses paragraphs to break up and organize larger ideas. The paragraphs (a) make sense, (b) avoid conceptual leaps, and (c) are used to explore or support an idea.

__ 4. Word choice: The writer (a) uses an academic writing style, (b) avoids speech-isms or colloquialisms, and (c) makes pragmatic choices about the quantity and quality of words.

__ 5. Headings: The writer uses headings to organize the paper and make it reader friendly. All the information under a particular heading is germane to that section.

__ 6. Quotes and citations: The writer uses APA 6th edition form as described here. The quotes and citations are used intelligently to support the writer's ideas.

__ 7. Fluency: The piece flows and is easy to read. Ideas are described and supported.

__ 8. Structure/organization: Structure is used to help carry the ideas.

__ 9. Form/mechanics: The piece looks presentable. The spacing, margins, font, and headings are correct. Spelling, grammar, and punctuation have been attended to.

10. Strengths of this paper:

11. Questions or areas to reconsider:

Key: 3 = very much, 2 = some, 1 = little, 0 = not at all

there is no calling it back. Thus, it is very important that you spend sufficient time and energy in the revising and editing phases.

THE FINAL WORD

Here are four big ideas to keep in mind as you begin the journey toward improved academic writing: First, initial drafts are works in progress. A good draft contains bad writing. Second, bad writing is the first step toward good writing. Celebrate badness as an important first step toward goodness. Third, you are neither a good writer nor a bad writer. You are a writer with the potential for both good and bad writing within you. Good writing will appear if you adhere to the process. Bad writing will appear if you take shortcuts. And finally, there is no such thing as a perfect paper.

II

Some Particulars of Academic Writing

Chapter Six

The Basics of Academic Writing

Academic writing is not speech written down. It is more formal, precise, purposeful, and objective.

All successful academic writers follow, to varying degrees, the steps described in the first five chapters of this book. These steps are recursive, meaning that some steps are repeated. Attention is now shifted slightly to focus on what the academic writing product should look like; however, there will be plenty of process tips sprinkled in along the way.

ELEVEN BASIC FUNDAMENTALS

The following are 11 basic fundamentals for academic writing:

1. *Provide just the facts.* The academic writer should take an objective stance to the greatest extent possible. Readers should be given just the facts and trusted to come to an apt conclusion based on the presentation (see Chapter 7). A certain amount of subjectivity will always exist simply in determining which facts are included and how they are explained; however, the academic writer should strive to be objective and unseen.

2. *Include only necessary information.* Too much information on the page can impede understanding. Thus, what is not included is just as important as what is included. Both objectivity and conciseness are to be valued.

3. *Do not use useless adjectives.* Adjectives add vitality to creative writing; however, too many adjectives in academic writing creates subjectivity and diminishes credibility.

4. *Do not use contractions.* Contractions should be eliminated from academic and professional writing.
5. *Font*: 12 point.
6. *Font face*: Times or Times New Roman (although this may vary).
7. *Margins*: One inch on the top, bottom, and sides.
8. *Line spacing*: Use double spacing between all text lines of the manuscript. Do not include extra spaces between sections or headings.
9. *Spacing between sentences*: Double spaces.
10. *Alignment*: Papers should be aligned flush left only. Do not use full alignment where margins are aligned on both the right and left sides. This creates uneven spacing between the words.
11. *Indentation*: The beginning sentence of all new paragraphs should be indented a half inch. Be consistent throughout. Block paragraphs should not be used. (These are paragraphs that are single-spaced, flush left, with a space above and below them.)

PERSONAL PRONOUNS

No personal pronouns were used in the making of the previous section (*I, you, me, we, your*). Notice the effect. Excluding them completely creates a detached, clinical feeling. There are times when this is most effective. There are other times when you want to include the reader by using a second-person personal pronoun (*you* or *your*). It is recommended that you simply be aware of your use of personal pronouns (there are two personal pronouns in this sentence). In academic and professional writing, using fewer personal pronouns creates a more objective feel.

WRITING AND SPEECH

Academic writing should sound distinctly different from speech when read out loud. Because of its one-way nature, writing must be more orderly and precise than speech. Ideas must be explained and supported. Also, writing allows us to examine our thoughts so they can be analyzed, shaped, evaluated, edited, and sorted before they are delivered. However, once delivered, these thoughts become frozen in time. Finally, ideas conveyed in writing are absorbed differently from speech. We initially attend to written ideas in a linear fashion, but then we skip around the message, moving back and forth to review and reread as necessary.

In contrast, speech is impermanent and is usually done with at least one other human present (hopefully). Speech consists of shorter sentences and is less formal, and because you are able to see your audience and judge their reaction, you are able to make immediate adjustments, clarifications, or even retractions. With speech, we received ideas in a linear fashion; however, we must rely on short-term memory to examine previous ideas. Also with speech, context and nonverbal communication are just as important to the total message as are the words.

WIDE READING ENHANCES YOUR ABILITY TO WRITE

Wide reading is one of the best ways to prepare yourself to be an academic writer. Wide reading helps to develop an innate sense of the structure of the language. Is also enhances vocabulary, conceptual knowledge, word identification skills, fluency, and comprehension. Reading of any kind is helpful, but reading formal texts, magazines, newspapers, and informational books is the best.

GRAMMAR MINILESSON: *FROM* VERSUS *THAN*

Which is correct: (a) Writing is different from speech, or (b) Writing is different than speech? Obviously it is the first one because that is the one used earlier. In academic writing, *different from* is the correct form.

Different From

The word *different* is an adjective, but it is not a comparative adjective. That is, it does not compare one thing to another; rather, it denotes a condition of difference:

> I took a different road home.
> The room was different.
> The man asked for a different hotdog.

Different from means two or more entities are not the same. In academic writing, this is the correct form when you are stating the existence of dissimilarity. You are not comparing; rather, you are merely stating that a difference exists.

- Incorrect: Writing is different than speech.
- Correct: Writing is different from speech. (You are not comparing writing to speech; rather, you are stating that a difference exists.)

- Incorrect: Basketball is different than soccer.
- Correct: Basketball is different from soccer. (You are simply stating that a difference exists between these two entities.)

Than

The word *than* is used for comparison or with comparative adjectives. Comparative adjectives show one thing in relationship to another. The word *than* should follow a comparative adjective:

better than, bigger than, faster than, more important than, smaller than

Different than is sometimes used in nonacademic writing to compare a noun to a clause. A *clause* is a part of a sentence that contains a subject (or noun) and a predicate (verb or action) (see Chapter 15):

- Example: The campus is different than it was 20 years ago.
- Example: The scores were different than they were at the beginning of the year.

The word *than* serves as a conjunction, or connecting word, between the noun and the clause; however, this is technically incorrect. While these two examples may be grammatically correct, in academic writing, we must be technically correct.

- Technically correct: The campus is different from what it was 20 years ago.
- Technically correct: The scores were different from what they were at the beginning of the year.

THREE GRAMMAR TIPS

First, it is important to be aware of grammar and precision in terms of word use and punctuation; however, do not become so consumed with it that it stymies the writing process. Remember that editing for grammar and punctuation does not occur until Step 5 of the writing process. This is the stage in which is it most appropriate to focus on grammar.

Second, you are always going to have grammar miscues or errors in your writing. Even professional grammarians do not catch everything. Everybody needs an editor.

And finally, we do not write to create grammatically correct writing. We write to transmit ideas. Correct grammar is used to facilitate the precision of this transmission. Nobody reads a book or an article because of the great grammar it contains.

AVOID SPEECH-ISMS

Academic writing uses different words and has a different style from the oral communication you use in your everyday life. Be aware of this. Avoid the use of colloquialisms, popular expressions, or speech-isms in your academic writing. Following are examples of five common speech-isms to avoid. This is not a complete list. However, this is presented to enhance your awareness of the words used in your academic writing:

1. "As likely as not"

   - Less effective: This will as likely as not create many questions.
   - More effective: This will likely create many questions.

2. "I can tell you that"

   - Less effective: I can tell you that this chemical should not be ingested.
   - More effective: This chemical should not be ingested.

3. "I might add that"

   - Less effective: I might add that this substance is toxic.
   - More effective: Also, this substance is toxic.

4. "It should be pointed out that"

   - Less effective: It should be pointed out that this article was written in 1928.
   - More effective: This article was written in 1928.

5. "Without a doubt"

   - Less effective: This was, without a doubt, the most important part of the article.
   - More effective: This was the most important part of the article.

AVOID NONWORDS

A nonword is one that does not need to be there. If a word is not needed, then do not use it. Too many words get in the way of your message:

Less effective: Basically, the chemical should not have been included in breakfast cereal.
Less effective: In essence, the chemical should not have been included in breakfast cereal.
Most effective: The chemical should not have been included in breakfast cereal.

THE LAST WORD

Accuracy, precision, and efficiency are the signs of effective academic writing.

Chapter Seven

Use Objective, Precise Language

Academic writers should be seen and not heard. Get out of the way. Let the data speak.

This chapter examines the use of objective language in your academic writing. The objective stance creates a more credible presentation than does a subjective rant; thus, it should be used when presenting information as well as when writing persuasive essays.

OBJECTIVE IS MORE PERSUASIVE THAN SUBJECTIVE

Academic writing should never (under any circumstance) sound like the discussions you hear on FOX or MSNBC television. Instead, ideas should be presented using concise, objective language. Even though one's position may be highly subjective, academic writers should strive to appear to be an unbiased presenter of information. This creates a more persuasive argument than does a strongly worded rant. For example, look at the following paragraph:

- Less Effective: With her outrageous $12.6 billion education bill, Governor Smith is boasting that her comical plan for educational reform will "embrace higher standards, innovation, and accountability." However, innovation and reform mean doing things differently. Sadly, Governor Smith is promoting the same old test-and-measure mentality based on whimsy and not on what research informs us is best educational practice.

Now compare this to the following example:

- More Effective: The governor's $12.6 billion education bill requires schools to implement more standardized tests. These will be used to determine the effectiveness of teachers and schools. However, this practice is not aligned with what a body of research has described as best practice.

The second paragraph makes the same points as the first without the hyperbole. It contains just the statements and supporting ideas. Opinions do not get in the way of the ideas. A subjective opinion is presented in an objective way, and thus, it enhances the possibility that a reader may be persuaded. Objectively stated arguments allow for the objective processing of that information. Subjective rants create emotional responses that, while impactful, are not always persuasive.

Avoid Letter-to-the-Editor Syndrome

Letter-to-the-editor syndrome is where highly charged statements and emotional buzzwords are used to convey a message. This style of writing weakens the argument and persuades only those who are already persuaded. In other words, those who agree with your position will continue to agree, those who are still deciding will be put off, and those who disagree will increase their resistance to your message.

- Less Effective: I really believe the school board has gone completely over the edge. They are forcing all elementary teachers to use the nutty new skills-based phonics program for their reading instruction. What are they thinking? This demonstrates just how ignorant and out of touch they are. Time after time, research has shown that there is no single method that works best for all students and that a balanced approach to reading instruction works best. Yet these monkeys, having read one article in a magazine, think they know more than the intelligent, creative teachers and professors who have spent years teaching and studying research related to literacy.

Concise, well-supported statements create a more powerful and persuasive argument than biased, hyperbolic language:

- More Effective: A body of research shows that there is no single method for reading instruction that works best for all students. If teachers are able to make instructional decisions in their classrooms, then they will be able to adapt instruction to the particular needs of their students.

Statistics Do Not Have Emotional Capacities

Statistics, results, implications, or actions are neutral events. Only the reaction of humans should be given an emotional status or described using an adjective. For example, the following statistic is not startling; it is simply a statistic. A person can be startled by the statistic, but by itself, a statistic, like a result, implication, or action, is a neutral event.

- Less Effective: A study by Jones (2009) reveals a startling statistic: Only 12% of teachers allow students to choose the books they want to read for reading instruction.
- More Effective: A study by Jones (2009) showed that only 12% of teachers allow students to choose the books for reading instruction. Allowing student choice will enhance motivation and increase voluntary reading.
- More Effective: A study by Jones (2009) showed that only 12% of teachers allow students to choose the books for reading instruction. This may be why some students tend not to feel motivated to read.

Avoid Should Statements

A should statement is where you say what you believe would be the right course of action without offering support. That is, you simply tell your readers what they must, should, or ought to do. You can strengthen your statements by avoiding such value words as *must, should,* and *needs to be.* Instead, state the idea, and support it.

- Less Effective: Teachers really should use reading workshop.

Why? Why should teachers use reading workshop? Is it just because you say so? Sorry, but that is not reason enough. Instead, strengthen the statement by saying it and supporting it with a reason (say it and support it).

- More Effective: Using reading workshop will enable teachers to provide multilevel instruction and meet the needs of all students.

Notice in the following examples how the more effective sentence in each case makes a statement and then supports it:

- Less Effective: All educators need to use a holistic approach to literacy instruction.
- More Effective: Using a holistic approach to literacy instruction will provide educators with an enhanced array of pedagogical tools.

- Less Effective: Academic writers must read and take careful notes before attempting a first draft.
- More Effective: Reading and taking careful notes before you begin the first draft will enable you to write more effectively with less time and effort.

However, if you are going to use a should statement, it will be more effective if followed by a supporting statement:

- Academic writers should use objective, academic language. This creates a more powerful argument than does a subjectively worded diatribe.

Using the graphic organizer in Figure 7.1 can help you avoid should statements. Write the original statement in the top box. Then generate two to five reasons to support the statement. From this you can create logical, consistent sentences or paragraphs and, at the same time, avoid should statements.

GRAMMAR MINILESSON: PERSONAL PRONOUNS

Personal pronouns are described briefly in Chapter 6. A personal pronoun takes the place of a person or people. Just like other pronouns, personal pronouns are used to avoid repetition. This reduces the clumsiness and enhances the readability of a sentence. For example, in the second sentence, *he* takes the place of *Bill*:

- Without a pronouns: Bill eats grapes. Bill also likes bananas.
- With a pronoun: Bill eats grapes. He also likes bananas.

Types of Personal Pronouns

There are three categories of personal pronouns: first person, second person, and third person (see Table 7.2). Avoid the use of first-person personal pronouns in your academic writing (some exceptions are described later). Make the writer disappear so that the ideas can speak. It is difficult to see the ideas on the page if the writer keeps bumping into you:

- First-person personal pronouns: I recommend that we increase the number of variables studied.
- Without pronouns: The number of variables studied must be increased.
- Without pronouns: Increasing the number of variables studied will enhance statistical accuracy.

Feel the following difference as we transition from the various pronoun stances:

Figure 7.1   Support-a-Statement Graphic Organizer

Statement:

Supporting reasons:
1.
2.
3.

Table 7.1   Types of Personal Pronouns

	Singular	Plural
First Person: The person or people are writing.	I, me	we, us
Second Person: The person or people are being written to.	you, your	you, your
Third Person: The person or people are being written about.	she, he, her, him	they, them

- First-person personal pronouns: I think buying Andy's book will enable us to become excellent academic writers.
- First-person personal pronouns: We need to buy Andy's book so that we can become excellent academic writers.

- Second-person personal pronouns: You need to buy Andy's book so that you can become an excellent academic writer.
- Second-person personal pronoun: Buying Andy's book will enable you to become an excellent academic writer.

- Third-person personal pronoun: Buying Andy's book will enable them to become excellent academic writers.
- Third-person personal pronoun: They are excellent academic writers because they bought Andy's book.

- Without pronouns: Buying Andy's book will enable people to become excellent academic writers.
- Without pronouns: Buying Andy's book will result in excellent academic writing.
- Without pronouns: The high quality of academic writing is related to the purchase of Andy's book.

Objective and Extremely Objective

Extreme objectivity can be achieved by removing all personal pronouns from academic writing. Compare the first paragraph to the second:

- Objective: In your academic writing, create sentences that state your idea, and then support it. This will help you avoid the use of should statements. A should statement is where you say what you believe would be the right course of action without offering support. That is, you tell your readers what they must, should, or ought to do. Even if a sentence does reflect your values, it can be made stronger by taking out such value words as *must, should*, and *needs to be*. Instead, state the idea, and support it.
- Extremely objective: Academic writing should contain sentences that state an idea and then support it. This will help to avoid the use of value statements. A value statement is where the writer describes a belief without offering support. That is, the reader is told what must, should, or ought to be done. Even if a sentence reflects the writer's values, it can be made stronger by taking out such value words as *must, should*, and *needs to be*. Instead, the idea should be stated and supported.

The extremely objective stance is often effective when writing something that may be controversial. Including personal pronouns creates writing that feels more connected with your reader. One style of writing is no more correct than the other. However, when in doubt, remove or severely limit the use of personal pronouns in your academic writing.

THE SUBJECTIVE STANCE

There are some instances where the subjective stance is appropriate. These are described here.

The Essay

In some essays, your thoughts, experiences, and perspectives are an integral part of the paper. Thus, such personal pronouns such *I*, *me*, and *my* may be used; however, limit their use. This enables the ideas and information to make your case and results in a stronger presentation.

Your Research

When you are reporting your own study, you can refer to yourself instead of "the researcher." Both are acceptable; however, for more formal quantitative research the objective is preferred:

- Subjective: For this study, I was looking for a school in a rural setting.
- Objective: For this study, the researcher was looking for a school in a rural setting.

Qualitative Research Methods

In qualitative research, the researcher becomes the lens through which a bit of reality is interpreted (see Chapter 22). In these instances, the researcher states any biases up front, describes how data were collected, presents the data, and makes conclusions based on the data. The researcher here is an important part of the research, and it is appropriate to use first-person personal pronouns as well as a subjective stance. However, credibility in these instances is maximized by presenting yourself as an unbiased observer to the greatest extent possible.

Writing About Your Experiences

In writing about your own experiences, you would, of course, include yourself.

Using Anecdotes or Observations

Sometimes, you can create a stronger paper and make a point come to life by including your experiences, insights, or anecdotes. These instances are rare in academic writing.

When in Doubt

When in doubt about using the objective or subjective stance, it is usually better to err on the side of eliminating all first-person personal pronouns from your writing. As described previously, this creates a more powerful document by letting the reader see the ideas instead of seeing you.

GRAMMAR MINILESSON: ADVERBS

An adverb is a word that modifies or expands on a verb, an adjective, another adverb, or a phrase. Its sole purpose is to alter or enhance what you have already written. The best advice is to avoid them when you can. They tend to clutter or confuse. If your language is precise, then you do not need adverbs. However, if you must use them, then do so with caution.

Intensifying Adverbs

Intensifying adverbs are used to intensify adjectives. Two common intensifiers are *very* and *really*:

- With an intensifying adverb: It was a very important variable.
- Without an intensifying adverb: It was an important variable.

In the first sentence, the word *very* modifies *important*. It was not just an important variable; it was a very important variable. However, academic writing should be more precise than this. We do not know the exact quantity of *very*. For example, what is the specific quantity or degree of *very important* in comparison to just *important*?

- With an intensifying adverb: The new treatment was really long and painful.
- Without an intensifying adverb: The new treatment was long and painful.
- A precise statement: The new treatment lasted two weeks and was reported as being painful by participants.

In the first sentence, *long* and *painful* are adjectives. However, the writer of the first sentence felt that the treatment was more than just long and painful. Apparently, it was really long and really painful. However, the use of the intensifier in this instance creates subjectivity and a lack of precision. The second statement is better. The last statement is the most precise and accurate. It reports the exact duration of the treatment and lets the reader determine if it was long or short. Also, unless the writer was a participant, that writer cannot testify to the pain of the treatment, only to what participants reported.

Qualifying Adverbs

Adverbs are sometimes used to qualify an adjective or verb. In the following first sentence, the word *almost* qualifies the word *always*; however, this qualifier lacks precision. If possible, strive for accuracy and precision:

- With a qualifying adverb: The treatment was almost always successful.
- Inaccurate example: The treatment was successful the majority of time.
- A precise example: The treatment was successful 95% of the time.

Degree-Enhancing Adverbs

Sometimes adverbs are used to enhance the degree to which something is or is not. They are used to add subtle editorial comment to what should be an objective sentence. Examples of degree-enhancing intensifiers are words like *amazingly*, *extremely*, *incredibly*, *really*, *remarkably*, *sadly*, *super*, *unbelievably*, and *very*. Do not use these!

- Nonacademic writing: Incredibly, the students did not make any academic gains.

Simply present the information and let the reader decide what is or is not incredible, amazing, or sad:

- Academic writing: The student did not make any academic gains.

The more degree-enhancing adverbs you use, the further you travel from precise, objective, academic writing:

- Without a degree-enhancing adverb: He was unprepared for the exam.
- With one degree-enhancing adverb: He was really unprepared for the exam.
- With two degree-enhancing adverbs: Amazingly, he was really unprepared for the exam.
- With three degree-enhancing adverbs: Amazingly, he was really, very unprepared for the exam.

As you become increasingly familiar with the tone and voice used in academic writing, you will begin to notice the degree to which the spoken language you hear around you is laced with degree-enhancing adverbs:

- Example: He is really, really, super excited to begin using academic writing in all his projects.

The Appropriate Use of Adverbs

There are instances that call for their appropriate use. However, be mindful of your use, and employ them judiciously:

- Without an intensifying adverb: The program was exhausting.
- With an intensifying adverb: The program was extremely exhausting.

THE LAST WORD

This chapter describes some of the elements that can dilute the power and precision of your academic writing. These are:

- Letter-to-the-editor syndrome
- Assigning emotions to statistics, results, implications, or actions
- Should statements
- First-person personal pronouns
- Intensifying, qualifying, and degree-enhancing adverbs

Chapter Eight

Keeping It Simple

Nothing sounds quite as silly as somebody trying to sound smart.

It takes no special talent to create academic writing that is complex. All you have to do is throw a lot of big words at your topic, create overly complex sentences, dump information all over the page, and use subject-specific jargon. Anybody can do this. Textbooks and academic journals are often filled with this kind of writing. However, this is NOT the mark of an effective academic writer.

An effective academic writer, like an effective teacher, makes complex things seem simple. In your academic writing, always seek clarity, simplicity, and succinctness. The purpose of writing is not to show how smart you are, how much you know, or how many big words you can use; rather, it is to transmit an idea or convey meaning in the most efficient and effective way possible.

CREATE READER-FRIENDLY WRITING

Effective academic writers explain things in ways that enable readers to easily make sense of their writing. Following are five simple tips for creating simple, reader-friendly writing:

1. *Use as few words as possible.* All things being equal, fewer words are always preferred over more words.
2. *Use simple, precise words.* All things being equal, a simple, precise word is always preferred over a big $5 college word. Big words neither impress nor inform. Clarity and economy of expression do.

3. *Know your audience.* Develop a sense of audience. To whom are you writing? Remember, you are writing to communicate ideas to actual people. So who are these actual people? What might they know already? More important, what is it that you think your readers might not know? Is there information that may serve more to confuse than to inform? What information does not need to be included? In academic writing, what you do not include is just as important as what you do include.

4. *Connect new to known.* In introducing a new or unfamiliar topic, connect new information to what you believe to be known or familiar information. This creates a bridge with familiar landmarks for readers to use as they cross from the familiar to the unfamiliar. For example, in the following paragraph, the topic of qualitative research is introduced. The audience here consists of upper-level undergraduate or graduate-level students. While they might not be familiar with qualitative research, it is assumed that most will have heard of Charles Darwin, Jane Goodall, or Margaret Mead. This becomes the bridge:

> *Qualitative research* uses systematic observations in order to understand a phenomenon, condition, or situation. Methods used by qualitative researchers are very much like those used by Charles Darwin observing the origins of species on the Galapagos Islands, Jane Goodall studying gorillas in the wild, or Margaret Mead studying Samoan cultures. Examples of data collection in a qualitative research might include interviews, structured observations, surveys, checklists, audio or video recordings, artifacts, case studies, products, performances, or field notes.

5. *Use analogies.* Familiar analogies can be used to connect the new to the known. In the following paragraph, the concept of a theory is introduced. In science and research, a theory is often confused with a hypothesis. A familiar dot-to-dot picture is used as an analogy to bring clarity here:

> A *theory* is a way to explain a set of facts. Put another way, if reality were a dot-to-dot picture, then a theory would be a way to connect a set of data dots. However, varying theories connect different data dots in different ways, resulting in a wide variety of pictures and practices. Thus, varying theories, while based on a set of empirical data, can often advocate different teaching practices. An example of this would be behavioral learning theory and cognitive learning theory, both of which are based on solid empirical evidence.

Using analogies creates communication that supersedes words. In the previous paragraph, understanding the concept of a dot-to-dot picture enables the reader to automatically plug new information about theories into this known concept. The writing also becomes multimodal in that the reader is now able to use images as well as words in coming to understand the concept of a theory.

WRITE IN 3-D

When introducing a new topic, idea, concept, or practice, write in 3-D: define, describe, and demonstrate. For example:

- *Define. Splandering* is the practice of using PowerPoint presentations and behavior modification techniques to teach phonics skills to young children.
- *Describe.* Here the teacher identifies a set of letter sounds and uses PowerPoint to create visually attractive pictures to go along with these letter sounds. Behavior modification techniques are then integrated with the presentation in order to reinforce positive learning behaviors.
- *Demonstrate (or provide a real-life example).* During reading class, children are asked to sit in chairs in an upright position with their feet planted on the floor. The lights are turned off, and children are asked to focus on the screen in the front of the room as the teacher begins the presentation. As the presentation begins, students are given sugar cubes every time they respond correctly to a PowerPoint prompt. If students give an incorrect response or if their attention drifts, then they are given a mild electric shock.

By the way, there's no such thing as "splandering."

NUMERICAL ORGANIZING WORDS

Effective writers sometimes use numerical organizing words (NOWs) to help readers see the structure and follow along when there are several points to be made or when something is described in sequential order. When using NOWs, first tell how many points are to be made up front (see the following example). Then use the words *first, second, third,* and so on to begin each point. Numerical organizing words enable you to add a sentence or two of explanation or elaboration after each point without confusing the reader. For example:

- There are four reasons students should learn to write well: First, those who are able to present their ideas in an orderly and interesting fashion are likely to get better grades. These writers are viewed as knowledgeable, credible students. Second, writing can be used to help organize thinking. Putting ideas on paper allows writers to look at several items at one time without taxing short-term memory. Third, people are more apt to attend to writing that is concise and organized. And finally, effective writing and communicating skills make graduating students a more valuable commodity in the job market.

Note that *firstly*, *secondly*, and *thirdly* are not used because they are not real words. Also, if you have just a few items to present, then you can use other kinds of organizing words, such as *after*, *also*, *next*, *since*, and *while*. However, make sure the beginning of each sentence is varied. Do not start succeeding sentences with the same word or phrase:

- Less effective: There are five steps to use in getting a paper started: First, decide on a topic. Then, brainstorm to generate ideas. Then, look for groups or patterns to use in organizing your ideas. Then, arrange your ideas into groups. Finally, use the first draft to get all the ideas on paper.
- More effective: There are five steps to use in getting a paper started: First, decide on a topic. Then, brainstorm to generate ideas. Next, look for groups or patterns to use in organizing your ideas. After this, arrange your ideas into groups. Finally, use the first draft to get all the ideas on paper.

SAY IT AND SUPPORT IT

One final tip for keeping your writing simple and clear is to present a single idea and support or explain it before moving on to the next idea. A sentence with supporting or explaining sentences is what makes a paragraph (see Chapter 12). Unsupported sentences that seem to be randomly slapped together negatively impact understanding. The following is an example of randomness:

- Less effective: Prewriting is an important part of the writing process. Revising is the key to effective writing. But to write effectively, you must use objective, academic language. Anybody can write. Also, reading a lot helps our writing.

These are all lovely ideas, but the paragraph makes little sense. Instead, each one of these ideas should become a paragraph. The following is an example of a paragraph with supporting ideas:

- More effective: Using a prewriting strategy helps to create a better paper. These strategies allow writers to focus solely on generating ideas before trying to write or shape them. Often, during this idea-generation stage, writers are able to tap into their unconscious and generate ideas of which they were not consciously aware. Also, with a list of possible ideas on the paper, writers are often able to see the structure of their paper and, thus, write a more organized paper in a shorter amount of time. Those who experience writer's block usually have not used a prewriting strategy.

The support-a-statement graphic organizer described in Chapter 7 (Figure 7.1) can be used to assist you in creating paragraphs that support and explain your ideas.

LAST WORD

Again, what you do not included in your academic writing is just as important as what you include. Keep it simple. Remember, you are writing to communicate ideas, not to demonstrate how much you know.

Chapter Nine

Reducing Bias

The words we use matter greatly.

One of the goals of academic writing is to present your ideas as clearly as possible. Bias of any kind gets in the way of your message and diminishes your credibility. Also, reducing bias in your writing increases the chances that your message will be received without bias by your reader.

PERSON-FIRST LANGUAGE

Person-first language is used to portray people as people and not as labels or categories. The goal of person-first language is to preserve the integrity of the humans about whom you are writing. For example, using the term *learning-disabled students* would reduce people to a category. Instead, person-first language would use such terms as *people who are learning disabled* or *students with learning disabilities.* They are people first who happen to have a condition, trait, or characteristic; they are not their condition, trait, or characteristic. You would not refer to *redheads* as if they were a separate category of humans; rather, you would say *people with red hair.*

EXCEPTIONALITIES

Sometimes the word *disabilities* is used to describe a restricting or limiting condition. Do not use the words *handicap* or *handicapped.* Again, the general rule of thumb is to refer to people who have specific conditions; do not refer to conditions as if they were specific people. The following are some common terms related to exceptionalities:

- Incorrect: intellectually challenged, intellectually disabled, mentally retarded, mental retardation
- Correct: people with cognitive disabilities, students with developmental cognitive disability, students with developmental disabilities

- Incorrect: learning-disabled people, slow learner, retarded
- Correct: a person with learning disabilities

- Incorrect: brain damaged, brain injured
- Correct: people with traumatic brain injury

- Incorrect: confined to a wheelchair, cripple, disabled people, handicapped, invalid, physically challenged
- Correct: people with disabilities, person who uses a wheelchair, person with physical disabilities

- Incorrect: autistic children, the insane, the mentally ill, mental patient, a neurotic person, neurotics, psychotics
- Correct: children with autism, people with mental illness, people with neurosis, people with psychiatric illness

- Incorrect: blind person, blind people
- Correct: people who are visually impaired, person who is blind

- Incorrect: deaf and dumb, deaf-mute, deaf person
- Correct: persons who are deaf or hard of hearing, person who is deaf

- Incorrect: emotionally disturbed, emotionally or behaviorally disturbed people
- Correct: people with emotional disabilities, students with emotional/behavioral disorders

- Incorrect: an epileptic, a hemophiliac, a paraplegic
- Correct: boy who is hemophiliac, person with epilepsy, woman who is paraplegic

- Incorrect: normal classroom, normal family, normal people
- Correct: general education classroom, people without a disability, person who is nondisabled

NORMAL PEOPLE

Do not, under any circumstances, use the term *normal* when you are referring to people without disabling characteristics. There are no such things as normal people, normal classrooms, or normal families. *Normal* is statistical term. There are statistical norms and a normal range of test scores, but there is no such thing as a normal person. To indicate such would be to say others are abnormal. Instead, use the term *persons without a disability*. It is also acceptable in this case to use a double negative, such as *people who are nondisabled*. In education, use the term *general education classroom* instead of *normal classroom*.

LEP

English language learner (ELL) is preferred over the term *limited English proficient* (LEP) (even though this term is used by the federal government). LEP describes a group of people in terms of what they cannot do. Other terms to use include *people who are non-native speakers* or *students who are ELL*. The term *English as a second language* (ESL) learners has been used, but this is not always accurate because many students are non-native speakers where English might be their third or fourth language.

GENDER

Gender is different from sex. Sex refers strictly to the biological dimensions of being male or female. Gender includes the sociocultural and psychological dimensions as well. In other words, one's gender identity refers to sexual differences that include the general parameters for acceptable behavior as established by society, peers, and one's family and the sociocultural context that describes what it means to be male or female.

Three Rules

The following are three rules that can help you create writing that is free of gender bias:

1. Whenever possible, use *man* to refer to a single male, and use *human* to refer to all of humanity. It is *humankind* rather than *mankind*. It is "One small step for humans" rather than "One small step for man." "All humans are created equal" rather than "All men are created equal."
2. Eliminate *man* as a designator of roles or categories whenever possible. For example: congressperson, chair or chairperson, news anchor, and firefighter. These have been the accepted forms for many years. In sports, it is a little trickier because of the years of tradition and male dominance. However, both males and females play most sports. To be accurate, we must also start thinking about our language here as well. In baseball or softball, it should be first baseperson rather than first baseman. In basketball, you throw the ball to the person in the post or the player in the post rather than the man in the post.
3. Never, *ever* use the male pronoun *he* when referring to both genders. This almost does not need to be addressed; however, it is mentioned here as a reminder because occasionally writers forget. To see how accustomed we have become to gender-neutral language, go to your library and look for a textbook written in the 1970s or before.

Simple Tricks to Avoid Gender Bias

The following are three tricks to use in avoiding gender bias in your writing.

Trick 1

Use plurals whenever possible.

- Incorrect: A writer must decide which prewriting strategy he will use.
- Correct: Writers must decide which prewriting strategy they will use. (Notice that *writers* is plural, so *they* must also be used because it is plural.)
- Better yet: Writers must decide which prewriting strategy to use.

Trick 2

Do not use pronouns.

- Incorrect: When a writer is beginning to write a report, he should make sure he has enough information.
- Correct: When beginning to write, it is important to have enough information.
- Better yet: It is important to have enough information before beginning to write.

Trick 3

Use *that person* or *people*.

- Incorrect: When a writer gets writer's block, he should use a prewriting strategy to generate ideas.
- Correct: When a writer gets writer's block, that person should use a prewriting strategy to generate ideas.
- Better yet: Using prewriting strategies to generate ideas will often eliminate writer's block.

Note: Using *s/he* or *he or she* should be avoided if possible, not because they are incorrect, but because they are messy and cumbersome.

SEXUAL ORIENTATION

"Sexual orientation refers to an enduring pattern of attraction, behavior, emotion, identity and social contacts" (APA, 2009, p. 74). The term *sexual orientation* should be used instead of *sexual preference*. The latter infers choice, and this is not the case in the majority of situations. Other terms to eliminate include *gender orientation* or *gender preference*. This infers that there is a monolithic block of people who all think and act the same way. The terms preferred are *gay men, bisexual men, lesbians*, and *bisexual women*. These are more accurate and preferred over the broader term *homosexual*. Reference to sexual orientation should be included in your writing only when pertinent.

LESBIAN, GAY, BISEXUAL, AND TRANSGENDER

LGBT (or *GLBT*) is a term that stands collectively for people who are lesbian, gay, bisexual, or transgender. *Transgender* refers to persons who identify or express a gender that is different from their sex at birth. The term *transsexual* sometimes gets confused with *transgender*. *Transsexual* refers to somebody who had gone through or is going through a medical procedure to change sex.

Transgender is a term used for people whose current gender or expression is different from their sex at birth. Terms related to people who are transgender continue to evolve. It has been described as both a category or noun and an adjective. When referring to a specific person, use *the person who is transgender* or *the transgender person*. When referring to groups, use *transgender community*, *transgender people*, or *people who are transgender*.

RACE AND ETHNICITY

Race refers to the classification of people according to specific physiological features or characteristics, such as hair or skin color; however, the word *ethnicity* is more often used in education. *Ethnicity* refers to a shared sense of identity or a pattern of characteristics based on nationality, race, religion, or language.

Preferences related to race and ethnicity change. In the past, terms used to refer to people of African ancestry living in North American have been *negro* or *Afro-American.* These terms have become dated. Most prefer *black* or *African American.* Three additional tips:

1. Racial and ethnic groups are designated by proper nouns. Thus, capitalize *Black* and *White* when referring to racial categories instead of *black* and *white*. However, in referring to a single white male, the term "white" is an adjective and not a proper noun.
2. Do not hyphenate multiword names. It is *Asian American* or *Mexican American*, not *Asian-American* or *Mexican-American.*
3. Other accepted terms include *American Indian, Asian, Hispanic, Indigenous People, Latino*, and *Native American*, or use the more specific subgroups, such as *Colombian, Cuban, Japanese, Vietnamese*, and so on.

FINAL WORD

Our language is constantly changing and evolving as new words appear and disappear from our cultural lexicon. In time, some of the terms here will most likely be replaced. However, words do matter. Lev Vygotsky (1962) describes words as tools of thought. They are used to manipulate ideas, to transform ideas, and to shape perception. The words we choose can be used to reinforce the commonality of the human experience and to recognize the dignity and worth of the individual human being. However, they can also be used to create a sense of other, to marginalize groups or objectivize people, or to present people as categories. Choose your words carefully and respectfully.

REFERENCES

American Psychological Association (APA). (2009). *Publication manual of the American Psychological Association* (6th ed.). Washington, DC: American Psychological Association.
Vygotsky, L. S. (1962). *Thought and language*. Cambridge, MA: MIT Press.

Chapter Ten

Avoiding Plagiarism

Plagiarism is always a bad idea.

Plagiarism is using somebody else's words, sentences, or ideas and claiming them to be your own. Do not do this. Ideas and intellectual integrity are the building blocks of higher learning and academic writing. In this context, plagiarism is the worst of all possible academic transgressions.

THE MOST EGREGIOUS EXAMPLE

The most egregious example of plagiarism would be to purchase an online research paper and submit it as your own or to pay an online service (or other another person) to write a paper for you. Textbox 10.1 contains information taken directly from the website *Advancedwriters.com*.

From Advancedwriters.com

Buy 100% Original Research Papers written by Professional Writers . . .

We searched high and low—we begged, we bargained, we pleaded, and now, we have over 600 expert writers—academic writers with Master's degrees and Ph.D.s in their fields. They work for us, but they are really only here to work for you. When you buy an original research paper online, you know the writer would not have sent it to you if they were not willing to turn in the work themselves.

Our writers are aware of the difficulties of meeting deadlines, and understand how months and months of classes can wear you down. That is why they will guarantee you on-time delivery of your custom research paper, error free, plagiarism free, and to your specific requirements.

The most important aspect of finding the right company to buy a research paper from, is knowing that the company will guarantee the work, and with unlimited free revisions, you know that your will be perfect and will get you the best grade possible.

Buying research papers online does not have to be difficult, doesn't have to make your life miserable, take a break this weekend and we will help you finish your research paper.

Using sources like these to write your paper is a bad idea for the following three reasons.

It Is Plagiarism

In the ultimate bit of irony, most of these sites claim to be "plagiarism free." However, the very act of paying somebody to write your paper for you and submitting it as your own is plagiarism. Even if you provide an outline and all the ideas, it is still plagiarism. Note the high moral tone taken in Textbox 10.2. SupremeEssays.com does not tolerate any kind of plagiarism, yet that is essentially what they do when they write your paper for you.

From SupremeEssays.com (n.d.)

Do you know how much can it effect on [*sic*] your academic performance? Most of the companies' [*sic*] providing custom writing services only rewrite old articles and term papers which can't be termed as 100% authentic. Moreover, you may even be charged with plagiarism if you submit such articles and essays in your college or university. But you can guarantee 100% original and unique essays and term papers when you order from us.

- Each of our essays and papers are checked with cutting age [*sic*] plagiarism detection tools which ensures that you get 100% unique writings
- We never deliver any article that has been compromised for plagiarism
- We do not tolerate any kind of plagiarism, copy/paste or paraphrasing

> We don't rewrite old articles or essays but rather put in our high quality writers to write essays manually using their own skill set. We have in-house plagiarism detection tool [*sic*] which scans all over the Internet to find any similar copies of essays. We don't use plagiarism detection tool [*sic*] offered by any third party as they may be outdated which can compromise the uniqueness of the articles. We check each of our essays twice for plagiarism before delivering it to you.
>
> Once the essays [*sic*] or term paper is submitted by our writer it directly goes into the automatic plagiarism detection tool and once this first phase is passed then the essay goes to our Expert Service department which checks the uniqueness manually. Our experts check each and every article to ensure you get 100% original essays and term papers.

However, it is acceptable (and preferable) to have somebody edit your final work. After you have completed all revisions, it is a good idea to have a classmate or colleague review your work to look for grammar, spelling, and punctuation errors that you and your computer did not catch or to provide feedback relative to clarity, structure, logic, and other issues that you did not see. This is commonly done by good academic writers but only at the very last stage. This is different from paying somebody to write your paper even if you provide the original ideas.

You Will Get Caught

There are many different software tools instructors can use to detect plagiarism (none that are divulged here). Also, most instructors have a fairly good sense of their students as writers and speakers through in-class conversations, in-class writing samples, online discussion groups, and chat sessions. If a paper suddenly appears that differs greatly in terms of vocabulary or sentence structure, then instructors may ask to see your notes and source materials. They might also compare your writing samples to the plagiarized paper. The penalties for plagiarism range from an automatic grade of F on the paper to course failure to suspension or expulsion from a college or university. Often there are no second chances.

It Deprives You of the Learning and Thinking Experience

You will not develop the writing skills that you need to succeed in future academic and professional endeavors. Also, you will not learn the thinking skills necessary for academic and professional writing, including (a) critical reading; (b) analyzing, synthesizing, and evaluating information; (c) inferring; and (d) extending and applying ideas.

OTHER EXAMPLES OF PLAGIARISM

Plagiarism again is using somebody else's words, sentences, or ideas and claiming them as your own. Some other examples of plagiarism include the following.

Cut and Paste

This is where sentences or even paragraphs are lifted from another source and inserted directly into your paper. With the variety of papers, articles, and websites available, this may seem like a tempting proposition; however, this type of plagiarism usually results in a paper that is disjointed and hard to read.

Not Citing Your Sources

Academic writing is based on the accumulation, analysis, and extension of other writers' ideas, constructs, theories, and research. It is okay to use these as long as you cite your sources. Chapter 18 describes how to cite your sources in text and on a reference page.

AVOIDING PLAGIARISM

Essays, academic articles, and research papers are built on information taken from books, journal articles, and other sources. So how do you avoid plagiarism? How do you make sure that you are not parroting the phraseology of another writer? Two simple tips: First, use the critical reading skills in Chapter 2. This will enable you to read for deep understanding and to perceive ideas and not just words and phrases. And second, use the note-taking strategies also in Chapter 2. Here, it is suggested that you record ideas using as few words as possible (short abbreviated sentences work best). This makes it more likely that you are recording ideas and not simply copying words and phrases. And then, when it comes time to write, you have to put these ideas into your own words for them to make sense.

THE LAST WORD

Academic writing is easy, as long as you follow the process. Trying to take shortcuts will always end up costing you more in terms of time and energy. This is a good place to review the steps in the academic writing process:

1. Research to gather data. Find sources, read, and take careful notes.

2. Use a predrafting strategy. Plan, create outlines, talk with others, generate ideas, or find structure.
3. Create a first draft. Make a first attempt to get some ideas on the page.
4. Revise. Reread, reshape, get feedback, and revise many times.
5. Edit. After your piece has gone through many revisions, look for spelling, punctuation, and grammatical errors.
6. Share. Send your writing out into the world.

REFERENCES

Advancedwriters.com. Retrieved from http://www.advancedwriters.com/
SupremeEssays.com (n.d.). *Plagiarism detection.* Retrieved January 1, 2016, from http://www.supremeessays.com/plagiarism.html

III

The Mechanics of Style for Academic Writing

Chapter Eleven

First and Last Paragraphs

Introductory paragraphs should introduce. Final paragraphs should highlight or summarize.

This chapter describes (a) introductory paragraphs, (b) seriation, and (c) last paragraphs.

THE INTRODUCTORY PARAGRAPH

Effective introductory paragraphs have two distinct purposes: First, they introduce the topic of the paper. Second, they provide the reader with a sense of structure related to the upcoming text. In its most basic form, an introductory paragraph would look like this:

CATS
This paper is about cats. Following are described (a) lions, (b) tigers, (c) leopards, and (d) lynx.

Introductory paragraphs should introduce, meaning that there should be just enough information to give the reader a sense of what the text is about and the areas to be covered. They are usually comprised of two to five sentences. The following is another example of an introductory paragraph. This is from the book *A Short Guide to Action Research* (Johnson, 2012):

Methods of Analyzing Data
This chapter describes data analysis. Analysis means to break something down into its component parts so that it can be understood. In action research, data are analyzed and organized into categories so that others might come to understand the reality you are trying to represent. Three elements related to data analysis are

presented in this chapter: (a) accuracy and credibility; (b) validity, reliability, and triangulation; and (c) inductive analysis.

In this paragraph, the first three sentences are used to give the reader some sense of what is contained in the chapter. The last sentence in the introductory paragraph uses seriation (described later) to delineate the structure of what is to follow. Another example:

THE IMPORTANCE OF ACADEMIC WRITING
In the world in which we currently exist, it is important to master the academic form of writing. This is because academic writing (a) shapes thinking, (b) represents us to others in an increasingly word-based, online reality, and (c) enables us to effectively and efficiently communicate important ideas.

This introductory paragraph uses just two sentences. Each of the points in the second sentence will then become a section in the paper:

THE IMPORTANCE OF ACADEMIC WRITING
In the world in which we currently exist, it is important to master the academic form of writing. This is because academic writing (a) shapes thinking, (b) represents us to others in an increasingly word-based, online reality, and (c) enables us to effectively and efficiently communicate important ideas.
Writing Shapes Thinking
Words are tools of thought. It can . . .
Our Online Persona
Increasingly, we communicate in cyberspace using only words. Other people make personal and professional judgments . . .
Efficient and Effective Communication
Academic writing is concise and objective. This provides the more efficient and effective way to communicate ideas using written words. It is . . .

There are three benefits to using this type of seriated sentence in your introductory paragraph: (a) It invites you to identify and use structure in your writing, (b) it enables the reader to see how the parts are related to the whole, and (c) it helps to create a smooth transition between sections (see Chapter 13). The following are specifics of seriation.

SERIATION

Seriation refers to organizing things in a series. Mastering the subtle art of seriation will enhance both your thinking and writing, and it enables you to clearly delineate your points. The following are seriation rules for using (a) commas; (b) letters and commas; (c) a colon, letters, and commas; (d) a semicolon, colon, letters, and commas, and (e) a colon, numbers, and paragraphs.

Commas Only

When you have three or more things in a list, use commas to separate them. Some sources say that a comma should not be used before the final *and* in a seriated sentence. Others say that *and* should be treated like any other item in a seriated sentence. Both are technically correct; however, for academic writing, Example B is the one that should be used:

- Example A: There are lions, tigers and bears in the forest.
- Example B: There are lions, tigers, and bears in the forest.

Letters and Commas

The official American Psychological Association (APA) rules of seriation state that, when listing three or more things in a series, you should use letters (not numerals) inside of parentheses to separate the ideas. (Make sure your parentheses are two-sided.) This type of seriation is very visual and enhances the comprehension of sentences that contain three or more ideas:

- Example: You can become an effective academic writer by (a) buying Andy's book, (b) studying Andy's video minilectures, or (c) paying Andy a lot of money to conduct a writing workshop.

Colon, Letters, and Commas

Use a colon when what follows extends or amplifies the preceding material:

- Example: You can become a better academic writer by doing any or all of the following: (a) buying Andy's book, (b) studying Andy's video minilectures, or (c) paying Andy a lot of money to conduct a writing workshop.

If the information that follows the colon is a complete sentence, then start this with a capital letter:

- Example: There are many ways to become an effective academic writer: You can (a) buy Andy's book, (b) study Andy's video minilectures, or (c) pay Andy a lot of money to conduct a writing workshop.

Semicolon, Colon, Letters, and Commas

When a series of items, ideas, or sentences have internal commas, use a semicolon to separate the items, ideas, or sentences. Both the following examples are correct; however, the letters inside the parentheses creates a more visually distinct presentation:

- Example: There are three things to consider about the movie *The Wizard of Oz*: There are no lions, tigers, or bears in the forest; Dorothy is kind, generous, and talented, but she kills two living beings; and the movie contains typical archetypal figures representing the shadow, the hero or heroine, and the wise sage.
- Example: There are three things to consider about the movie *The Wizard of Oz*: (a) There are no lions, tigers, or bears in the forest; (b) Dorothy is kind, sensitive, and forgiving, but she kills two living beings; and (c) the movie contains typical archetypal figures representing the shadow, the hero or heroine, and the wise sage.

Colon, Numbers, and Paragraphs

When each successive item or point becomes a paragraph, indent and use numerals to delineate each point. The numeral takes the place of the number words *first*, *second*, *third*, and so on:

• Example: There are three things to consider about the movie *The Wizard of Oz*:

1. There are no lions, tigers, or bears. The forest represents that unexplored part of unconsciousness of which we tend to be afraid. It is interesting to know that the Cowardly Lion is in fact a lion. Part of what we fear in exploring our inner landscapes is encountering and exposing our true selves.

2. Dorothy is a killer. In the movie, Dorothy is represented as a kind, sensitive, gentle girl from Middle America, yet she is the only character in this movie who kills. She kills the Wicked Witch of the East and steals her shoes. When the Wicked Witch of the West tries to reclaim what should have been rightfully hers, Dorothy kills her as well.

3. It contains archetypal characters. These characters represent parts of our psyche. For example, the witch is the classic shadow figure similar to Darth Vader in *Star Wars* or Lord Voldemort in *Harry Potter*.

Do Not Become Seriation Happy

Do not overuse this technique. If seriation is overused, then your paper will begin to sound like a series of lists. In the following example, seriation in the form of letters and parentheses are used in the introductory paragraph. Using it immediately in the subsequent section makes it feel clumsy and list-like. Again, this is an example of bad seriation:

Archetypal Elements in the Movies
This paper examines three archetypal elements of the movie *The Wizard of Oz*: (a) the classic journey theme, (b) the archetypical hero character, and (c) the struggle of good and evil.

Journey Theme
Journey themes have been used throughout literature, fairy tales, and movies. Mythologist Joseph Campbell describes four central ideas common to this type of mythology: (a) the hero travels from home, goes to a foreign land, fights evil, attains new power, and returns home stronger than when he or she left; (b) the hero attains

new strength, wisdom, or powers; (c) there is an encounter and a struggle against evil; and (d) the hero returns home a better and more powerful human.

Traveling From Home

A hero might travel from home in various ways or for various reasons: (a) in search of adventure, (b) on a religious quest, (c) by accident, or (d) against his or her will.

THE LAST PARAGRAPH

The last paragraph (sometimes the last two paragraphs) should be used to summarize or highlight focal ideas previously described. It can also be used to link, extend, or apply ideas previously stated. Do not introduce any new material here. If this chapter were an academic article, then the last paragraph would look something like this:

In academic writing, use the introductory paragraph to introduce what you will be writing about. Seriation can be used to delineate these elements and provide a preview of the upcoming text. Seriation is also a useful tool to use occasionally within the body of your writing. Finally, use the last paragraph to summarize or highlight the main ideas or to extend and apply ideas.

REFERENCE

Johnson, A. (2012). *A short guide to action research* (4th ed.). Boston: Allyn and Bacon.

Chapter Twelve

Paragraphs Are Our Friends

Readable writing is more likely to be read.

A paragraph is a group of sentences organized around a similar idea. Paragraphs are our friends. They create a physical break between one idea and the next. They also help us to organize our thinking as we are writing, and they enable the reader to better perceive the structure of our writing. Without paragraphs, your text becomes a big blob of words that can be very hard to read. The following is an example of an unpublished text without paragraphs:

Along with creativity, intuition has also been an important element in some of humankind's outstanding innovations and breakthroughs. Intuition is a cognitive function, something our brains do naturally (whether you are aware of it or not). It is a type of thinking that is nonlinear as well as a level of awareness or state of consciousness. Intuition is defined here as a sudden knowing apart from logic or knowledge. It is the ability to make the leap from the known or predictable to something totally different. It also involves realigning known information in totally new ways. There are three levels or types of intuition: rational intuition, predictive intuition, and transformational intuition. Rational intuition is thinking that realigns known information. It is that "aha" experience where you sudden see the solution to a problem or get new insight. Often new information is combined with forgotten information to connect the dots in a different way. This type of awareness seems to come when you are sleeping or when your mind is relaxed or thinking of other things. Predictive intuition is thinking that utilizes known information to form new patterns, sequences, ideas, or plans. Here, you use information to create a hunch, guess, or hypothesis. You are able to perceive the whole based on only partial information. Again, this is something the brain naturally does. Your brain naturally uses partial data and completes the picture. Transformational intuition is thinking or awareness that uses a different kind of sensing to pick up information. This defies most traditional scientific explanations. Here, information seems to come from a source outside the individual. This can also be the type of B-cognition described by Abraham Maslow that often occurs when we are working or performing at our highest states during peak experiences (Maslow, 1971).

Nobody wants to read a blob of text like this. Now notice what happens when paragraphs are included to break up the text and separate the ideas:

Along with creativity, intuition has also been an important element in some of humankind's outstanding innovations and breakthroughs.

Intuition is a cognitive function, something our brains do naturally (whether you are aware of it or not). It is a type of thinking that is nonlinear as well as a level of awareness or state of consciousness. Intuition is defined here as a sudden knowing apart from logic or knowledge. It is the ability to make the leap from the known or predictable to something totally different. It also involves realigning known information in totally new ways.

There are three levels or types of intuition: rational intuition, predictive intuition, and transformational intuition.

Rational intuition is thinking that realigns known information. It is that "aha" experience where you sudden see the solution to a problem or get new insight. Often new information is combined with forgotten information to connect the dots in a different way. This type of awareness seems to come when you are sleeping or when your mind is relaxed or thinking of other things.

Predictive intuition is thinking that utilizes known information to form new patterns, sequences, ideas, or plans. Here, you use information to create a hunch, guess, or hypothesis. You are able to perceive the whole based on only partial information. Again, this is something the brain naturally does. Your brain naturally uses partial data and completes the picture.

Transformational intuition is thinking or awareness that uses a different kind of sensing to pick up information. This defies most traditional scientific explanations. Here information seems to come from a source outside the individual. This can also be the type of B-cognition described by Abraham Maslow that often occurs when we are working or performing at our highest states during peak experiences (Maslow, 1971).

The inclusion of paragraphs in this example makes it much more readable and, thus, much more likely to be read and understood. Now notice what happens now when we include headings, subheadings, and bullet points:

Intuition
Along with creativity, intuition has also been an important element in some of humankind's outstanding innovations and breakthroughs.
What Intuition Might Be
Intuition is a cognitive function, something our brains do naturally (whether you are aware of it or not). It is a type of thinking that is nonlinear as well as a level of awareness or state of consciousness. Intuition is defined here as a sudden knowing apart from logic or knowledge. It is the ability to make the leap from the known or predictable to something totally different. It also involves realigning known information in totally new ways.
Three Levels of Intuition

There are three levels or types of intuition: rational intuition, predictive intuition, and transformational intuition.

• **Rational intuition** is thinking that realigns known information. It is that "aha" experience where you sudden see the solution to a problem or get new insight. Often new information is combined with forgotten information to connect the dots in a different way. This type of awareness seems to come when you are sleeping or when your mind is relaxed or thinking of other things.

• **Predictive intuition** is thinking that utilizes known information to form new patterns, sequences, ideas, or plans. Here, you use information to create a hunch, guess, or hypothesis. You are able to perceive the whole based on only partial information. Again, this is something the brain naturally does. Your brain naturally uses partial data and completes the picture.

• **Transformational intuition** is thinking or awareness that uses a different kind of sensing to pick up information. This defies most traditional scientific explanations. Here, information seems to come from a source outside the individual. This can also be the type of B-cognition described by Abraham Maslow that often occurs when we are working or performing at our highest states during peak experiences (Maslow, 1971).

Compare this last writing sample to the blob of writing at the beginning of the chapter. The sentences are identical in each. However, the use of paragraphs, headings, subheadings, and bullet points enables the reader to clearly see the structure of the text. This results in a much more readable text, which leads to a great truth in academic writing: Readable writing is more likely to be read.

WHEN TO START A NEW PARAGRAPH

Every paragraph should have a focus or central idea. A new paragraph should be started whenever you find yourself wandering into a new idea. When in doubt, create a new paragraph. Overparagraphed writing is much easier to read than underparagraphed writing. The one caveat here is that you want to avoid one-sentence paragraphs.

The following writing sample is about writer's block. The first paragraph introduces the concept of writer's block. The second paragraph starts explaining mental operations. A third paragraph was created when the author began writing about specific strategies for dealing with writer's block:

How to Avoid Writers' Block

Sometimes when attempting to write, the words and ideas just do not come out. And the harder you try, the fewer words and ideas appear on the page. This is commonly known as writer's block. This usually means that you are trying to get it just right the first time. You are trying to edit and generate ideas at the same time.

Writing involves two opposite mental operations: generating and evaluating. You need to generate in order to get an abundance of words and ideas, but you also need to evaluate in order to throw out words and reshape the ideas you have generated.

But you cannot do both operations at the same time. You cannot generate and evaluate simultaneously and expect to create anything but warm mush. The reason for this has to do with the way our brains work. While our long-term memory (LTM) can hold a great deal of information for an almost infinite duration, our short-term memory (STM), or working memory, can hold only about seven chunks of information for approximately 15 seconds. This is not much room for a great deal of information. If you try to edit and organize your ideas at the same time as you are generating ideas, then STM becomes overloaded, and many of the ideas seem to slip away or become scattered.

One of the best cures for writer's block is to use a pencil and a legal pad and write as quickly and as badly as possible (see "Power Writing" earlier). This technique allows you to bypass the little editor in your head so that you can get your initial ideas on paper. As described previously, editing is the last step in the writing process.

In general, putting the main point up front makes your paragraphs easier to read (which is the ultimate goal). This avoids making the reader wade through most of your paragraph to discover your point. Remember that a confused or frustrated reader soon becomes a nonreader. In the following, the main point is stated in the first sentence. All the sentences that follow are related to this main point:

> • Dorothy is the classic hero figure. She travels from one dimension to another. She battles evil. She journeys to find special powers and becomes transformed along the way. Finally, she returns home with new insight.

AVOID CONCEPTUAL LEAPS

A conceptual leap is where the writer suddenly leaps from one thing to another, leaving the reader struggling to find the bridge between the two. Conceptual leaps within paragraphs and between paragraphs are to be avoided.

> • Less effective: Creativity is a valuable cognitive process. Creativity is a type of problem-solving. Being able to perceive problems is an important part of creativity. Highly creative people are able to look at problems in different ways.

This paragraph contains some interesting ideas; however, instead of developing and supporting them, the writer jumps from one idea to the next. In the following, the writer develops each idea and transitions from one paragraph to the next (transition words and sentences are described in the next chapter). The topic of creativity is the unifying element here. Each paragraph explores a different aspect of creativity:

- **More effective:** Creativity is a valuable cognitive process. It is a trait that has helped to produce important innovations and solve some of our most complex and compelling problems. Creativity is a type of thinking that enables people to generate new ideas, improve old ideas, and recombine existing ideas in a novel fashion. It is the ability to transcend traditional ways of thinking.

   Creativity is a type of problem-solving. Problems can be found in all areas, including the arts, business, science, sports, and even education. For examples, how can we design a car to run on electricity? How can this feeling or idea be expressed through movement, dance, music, or visual art in a way that entertains? What kind of a play will enable our team to score a touchdown? How can I make this relationship work? How can this concept be explained so that people understand it? These are all problems that require creative thinking for their ultimate solution.

   Being able to perceive problems is also an important part of creativity. You cannot solve a problem unless you are aware of it. A problem is a difference between the current and ideal state. Creative individuals are able to sense this difference (between what is and what could be).

   Another trait that enables highly creative people to solve problems is their ability to look at them in different ways. This is called redefining the problem. Creative problem-solvers are able to let go of the old ways of thinking, which in turn enables them to generate a variety of novel solutions. This is the "thinking outside the box" cliché with which you are most likely familiar. By freeing themselves from conventional ways of thinking and by examining problems from a variety of angles, highly creative people open themselves up to a variety of new possibilities.

In this example, the salient point is stated first in each paragraph, while the remaining sentences are used to support, explore, or elaborate these ideas.

APPROPRIATE LENGTH OF A PARAGRAPH

The appropriate length of a paragraph is this: long enough to develop the idea and short enough to prevent the reader from becoming bored or confused. More complicated ideas require larger paragraphs; less complicated ideas require smaller paragraphs. Again, strive to keep your academic writing as concise as possible. What you do not include in a paragraph is just as important as what you do include.

AVOID REDUNDANCY WITHIN A PARAGRAPH

In general, state an idea only once in a paragraph. Repeating an idea clutters up your writing and adds to the confusion:

- **Less effective:** In academic writing, the most effective way to make a strong case for your particular point of view is by using objective language and sound reasoning. Even though your position may be highly subjective, you should strive to appear unbiased in your presentation of information. Logical arguments using objective language is the most effective way to support your position, not subjective language, emotional buzzwords, or hyperbole.

This writer wants to stress the importance of objective language and sound reasoning; however, restating the same idea differently does little to make the original idea a better one.

• More effective: In academic writing, the most effective way to make a strong case for your particular point of view is by using objective language and sound reasoning. Even though your position may be highly subjective, strive to appear unbiased in your presentation of information. This creates a much stronger argument.

AVOID REDUNDANCY WITHIN THE PAPER

Finally, avoid redundancy within your paper. If you have stated an idea in another place, then you may refer to it, but it should not be presented as something new. The reader does not know if you are introducing a new idea or if a similar idea was misread when it was first encountered. If you must restate something, then use clue words like *again* to let the reader know that this idea has appeared before. Other phrases to use here include *as stated previously*, *once again*, *to reiterate*, or *to repeat*. For example, "Again, it is important to avoid redundancy."

THE LAST WORD

Paragraphs are our friends. Embrace your friends.

REFERENCE

Maslow, A. (1971). *The farther reaches of human nature.* New York: Viking Press.

Chapter Thirteen

Transition Words and Sentences

Good academic writing reads like melted butter.

MINIMIZING CONCEPTUAL LEAPS

The last chapter describes how conceptual leaps between sentences can leave the reader confused and disrupt comprehension. Transition words and phrases can minimize this. Transition words and phrases can be used to (a) signal a change in idea, (b) show how one idea relates to another, and (c) help the reader see the logical sequence of ideas.

Transition words provide a variety of cues for the reader. The following are various categories and related transition words:

- To show contrast: but, conversely, however, in contrast, instead, nevertheless, nonetheless, notwithstanding, on the contrary, otherwise, still, though, yet
- To denote time or connectivity: additionally, after, again, also, and, as well, as well as, at last, before, besides, formerly, last, later, meanwhile, next, previously, since, then, too
- To show summary: consequently, finally, in conclusion, therefore, thus, to sum up
- To connect: additionally, after, again, also, and, as well as, before, besides, finally, formerly, further, in addition, last, later, next, previously, since, then, too
- To show cause and effect: accordingly, although, because, consequently, for that reason, hence, however, since, so, thereafter, therefore, thus, whereas
- To show similarities: as, as well, in like fashion, just as, like, likewise, similarly, similar to
- To show differences: although, but, even so, however, instead, on the contrary, otherwise
- To denote examples: for example, for instance, in particular, meaning that, specifically, thus, to illustrate

- To add more information: also, and, as well, besides, further, furthermore, in addition, likewise, moreover, not only . . . but also
- To show argument or concession: admittedly, certainly, consequently, despite, despite the fact that, even so, furthermore, however, in fact, nevertheless, of course, undoubtedly, yet
- To show a result: as a consequence, consequently, hence, so, subsequently, therefore, thus

Transition phrases are generally used at the ends and beginnings of paragraphs to minimize conceptual leaps. They create a more coherent and unified piece of writing, connecting previous ideas to new ideas. This is illustrated in the following unpublished text, where the transition sentences are bold-faced:

Reality

If you look deep enough, then you see that there is no difference between reality and fantasy, subjective and objective, the idea and the thing. All are variants of the same reality. All are waves, temporary forms consisting of the same water.

Thich Nhat Hanh (1999), the Buddhist mystic, describes two levels of reality that exist simultaneously: *Phenomenal reality* is the reality of things seen, that which we are used to seeing and experiencing. These are the waves, bits of reality coming into temporary form. This reflects the objective outer world, where truth is determined by repeatability and the laws of cause and effect. Noumenal reality is the reality inaccessible to logic or the normal senses. This is the water, the essence of all things, the ground of all being. This reflects the subjective inner world, where truth is determined by meaning.

Plato used the allegory of a cave to explain these two dimensions of reality. According to the allegory, we live inside a cave. Those things that appear in the physical world as real to us (phenomenal reality) are only shadows on the wall of this cave caused by the sun shining on the true things outside (noumenal reality). Everything inside the cave is temporary.

You may look at the chair you're sitting on and say, "Wait a minute, how can this be? This chair is not temporary. It's right here, and I'm sitting on it." But even as you sit, that chair is in a state of decay. Someday, the chair as you know it will be like the wave that has crashed on the shore. Its form will be dissipated and its parts scattered. Thus, the chair is real but a very temporary manifestation.

More permanent manifestations reside outside the cave. Here, the outer is the inner. This is the subjective world of invisible ideas where the sun shines. Noumenal reality is the realm where the authenticity of phenomena is determined by connotation or what it suggests rather than denotation or what attributes it consists of. Consequently, those images that appear to us here are absolutely real and authentic insofar as we can determine their meanings.

The very transitory nature of what we call the physical realm and its relation to time is described aptly by Stephen Hawking (1988) in *A Brief History of Time*. Think of a puddle of milk spilled on a tabletop and spreading outward as the beginning of what we know as phenomenal reality. However, instead of two dimensions, think of it expanding in three dimensions like a balloon. As this puddle expands outward, it becomes thinner. Thus, we are essentially fading away like the Cheshire cat. Hawking posits that reality as we know it is moving from perfect order (the pre-spilled-milk condition) to chaos (spilled milk and beyond).

So in terms of inner or outer, subject or objective, one is no more real than the other; however, one is more permanent. Thus, Plato, Buddha, St. Paul, and Jesus all stressed ideas or ideals, such as personal virtues, consciousness, compassion, understanding, and harmonious relations among the facilities of the soul, for these are eternal things.

USING SERIATION TO FACILITATE TRANSITIONS

Smooth transitions can also be facilitated through the use of seriation (see Chapter 11) and headings (see Chapter 14). Notice how the last sentence of the following first paragraph alerts the reader to look for three types of connections. This is followed by three headings with bullet points to delineate these. Seriation used effectively can eliminate the need for transitions.

Finally, the principle of interconnectedness is manifest in a holistic education framework in the design of curriculum and other education experiences (Johnson, 2006). These are used as vehicles to develop three kinds of connections: intrapersonal connections, interpersonal connections, and transpersonal connections:
• Intrapersonal connections: Curriculum and other educational experiences are used to connect with and understand the central self. The central self is the part of you beyond the ego that some might call the soul. Intrapersonal connections can help students to understand themselves, solve problems, make decisions, and come to know the world using intuition and emotion in conjunction with knowledge and logic.
• Interpersonal connections: Curriculum and other educational experiences are used to connect with and understand others. Interpersonal connections can help students develop social and other interpersonal skills with the goal of understanding and learning to live in relationship or harmony with others.
• Transpersonal connections: Curriculum and other educational experiences are used to perceive and understand the world in terms of interrelated systems and interconnected experiences. This might take the form of global education, where students see how their daily lives affect or connect with others around the world. This might also take the form of ecological education, where students describe their impact on and relationship with the environment.

THE LAST WORD

As stated previously, good academic writing reads like melted butter. Transition words and phrases can be used toward this end.

REFERENCES

Hawking, S. W. (1988). *A brief history of time: From big bang to black holes*. New York: Bantam Books.

Johnson, A. (2006). *Making connections in elementary and middle school social studies.* Thousand Oaks, CA: Sages.

Nhat Hanh, T. (1999). *Going home: Jesus and Buddha as brothers.* New York: Riverhead Books.

Chapter Fourteen

Headings and Subheadings

Use headings and subheadings to make the organizing structure of your writing abundantly clear.

Headings and subheadings are used to show the structure of your text, thus making it easier to read. Three levels of headings are described here, but first, a demonstration of their effect. The following is a large blob of text without headings:

The Wizard of Oz

The Wizard of Oz is considered a classic. First released in 1939, it has endured for generations. This paper examines three elements that contribute to its success: It uses the classic journey theme, has an archetypical hero character, and involves a battle of good and evil.

Journey themes have been used throughout literature. Joseph Campbell describes this as the mythical journey. Here, the hero travels from home, goes to a foreign land, fights evil, attains new power, and returns home stronger than when the hero left. In *The Wizard of Oz*, Dorothy leaves Kansas and travels to another dimension. In this dimension, she encounters evil in the form of the Wicked Witch of the West. Her new powers are her ruby red slippers. When she returns to Kansas, she has new insight that will supposedly help her become a better human and live a happier life.

In this movie, Dorothy is the archetypical hero figure used throughout literature and mythology. Like Luke Skywalker, Buddha, Gilgamesh, Moses, and Jesus, there are questions regarding her parents. Why is she living with her aunt and uncle? What happened to Mr. and Mrs. Gale? Also, like most classical heroes, Dorothy has loyal companions who help her fight evil. Finally, Dorothy is the only character in the movie to take a moral stance. When the Cowardly Lion first appears, he begins chasing Toto around the tree. Not knowing he is cowardly, Dorothy risks her life by slapping the Cowardly Lion on the nose. She tells him it is wrong for those who are bigger and stronger to pick on the small and the weak.

The concept of evil is very clearly defined in this movie. Here, the Wicked Witch of the West clearly illustrates what Jung describes as our shadow or dark side. This is the part of our psyche, little explored, that houses our more base instincts. Much like the Satan figure in Christian mythologies and despots throughout history, the witch projects this shadow side with her need to conquer and control. Dorothy, however, is clearly good and might be considered a projection of our higher nature.

Section Headings

A large blob of text like this can feel fatiguing to read. Now watch the magic. Notice the difference when the same large blob of text is inserted with some section headings and an introductory paragraph on the front. Section headings (called Level 1 headings) are centered, bold-faced, with the first letter of the principle words capitalized. Writing starts on the next line:

The Wizard of Oz

The Wizard of Oz is considered a classic. First released in 1939, it has endured for generations. This paper examines three elements that contribute to its success: (a) the use of the classic journey theme, (b) the archetypical hero character, and (c) the theme of good versus evil.

Journey Theme

Journey themes have been used throughout literature. Joseph Campbell describes this as the mythical journey. Here, the hero travels from home, goes to a foreign land, fights evil, attains new power, and returns home stronger than when the hero left. In *The Wizard of Oz*, Dorothy leaves Kansas and travels to another dimension. In this dimension, she encounters evil in the form of the Wicked Witch of the West. Her new powers are her ruby red slippers. When she returns to Kansas, she has new insight that will supposedly help her become a better human and live a happier life.

Archetypical Hero

In this movie, Dorothy is the archetypical hero figure used throughout literature and mythology. Like Luke Skywalker, Buddha, Gilgamesh, Moses, and Jesus, there are questions regarding her parents. Why is she living with her aunt and uncle? What happened to Mr. and Mrs. Gale? Also, like most classical heroes, Dorothy has loyal companions who help her fight evil. Finally, Dorothy is the only character in the movie to take a moral stance. When the Cowardly Lion first appears, he begins chasing Toto around the tree. Not knowing he is cowardly, Dorothy risks her life by slapping the Cowardly Lion on the nose. She tells him it is wrong for those who are bigger and stronger to pick on the small and the weak.

Good and Evil

The concept of evil is very prevalent in this movie. Here, the Wicked Witch of the West clearly illustrates what Jung describes as our shadow or dark side. This is the part of our psyche, little explored, that houses our more base instincts. Much like the Satan figure in Christian mythologies and despots throughout history, the witch projects this shadow side with her need to conquer and control. Dorothy, however, is clearly good and might be considered a projection of our higher nature.

Subheadings

Now see how subheadings can be used to organize a section. Subheadings (sometimes referred to as Level 2 headings) are flush left, italicized, bold-faced, with the first letter of the principle words capitalized. Writing should start on the next line:

Good and Evil

The concept of evil is very prevalent in this movie. Here, the Wicked Witch of the West clearly illustrates what Jung describes as our shadow or dark side.

The Shadow Side

This is the part of our psyche, little explored, that houses our more base instincts. Much like the Satan figure in Christian mythologies and despots throughout history, the witch projects this shadow side with her need to conquer and control. Dorothy, however, is clearly good and might be considered a projection of our higher nature.

An Elusive Concept

Good and evil are not always easily defined. For example, in Kansas, Toto bites Miss Gulch. This is not a good thing, and Miss Gulch operates within the law in seeking to have Toto destroyed. Dorothy, on the other hand, allows her dog to wander unattended. Also, she tries to run away from home without considering her family, she steals shoes that are not her own, she kills two witches, and she eats apples that do not belong to her.

Indented Headings

Indented headings (Level 3 headings) can be used to organize and show the structure within a subsection. Level 3 headings are indented and bold-faced, only the first word is capitalized, there is a period at the end, and the writing starts on the same line.

An Elusive Concept

Good and evil are not always easily defined.

The law. In Kansas, Miss Gulch is following the law. Dorothy does not. Toto bites Miss Gulch. Miss Gulch operates within the law in seeking to have Toto destroyed. Dorothy, on the other hand, allows her dog to wander unattended.

Right and wrong. Dorothy's acts are immoral according to most traditions. She steals shoes that are not her own, she kills two witches, and she eats apples that do not belong to her.

Concern for others. Dorothy runs away from home without considering how her actions may affect her family. Also, Dorothy abruptly leaves Oz without considering how her absence affects the many Munchkins who have come to depend on her. Her sudden departure has the potential for mass chaos, rioting, and even starvation among the Munchkins and flying monkeys.

The three levels of headings described here should get you through most academic writing. In the following, the three levels are described and demonstrated:

Level 1 Headings
Level 1 headings (section headings) are centered and bold-faced, with the first letter of the principle words capitalized. Writing starts on the next line.
Level 2 Headings
Level 2 headings (subheadings) are flush left, italicized, and bold-faced, with the first letter of the principle words capitalized. Writing should start on the next line.
Level 3 headings. Level 3 headings (indented headings) are indented and bold-faced, the first word is capitalized, there is a period at the end, and writing starts on the same line.

THE LAST WORD

As stated previously, using headings enhances the readability of your text, as the reader can see the structure of your presentation and how one thing relates to another. And as has been stated many times in this text, finding and using an organizing structure will help in the writing of your paper, as it provides a map for arranging ideas and creating a logical flow of information. But not every text needs all three levels of headings. Often you need only Level 1 headings. Too many headings or too many levels of headings could get in the way. But here is an important point: If you find your text overheaded, then you can always remove some of your headings, and the structure will still be there. Thus, during the revision stages of your text, it is recommended that you err on the side of overheading rather than underheading.

Chapter Fifteen

Grammar

Riddle: How do you identify the indirect object of a prepositional phrase?
Answer: If you want to get any writing done, then you don't.

Correct grammar usage helps to create precision in writing and speaking. While you do not have to be a grammarian to write well, you should be familiar with some basic grammar rules and develop an intuitive sound for academic language. This chapter contains some tips for avoiding nine common grammatical errors. These should get you through most academic writing situations.

1. Stay consistent with tense. If you use a particular tense (past, present, or future) in the first part of a sentence or paragraph, then you must use it throughout:

- Incorrect: John read the paper and took a nap (past tense). He sleeps on the couch (present tense).
- Correct: John read the paper and took a nap. He slept on the couch (both use past tense).
- Correct: John reads the paper and takes a nap. He sleeps on the couch (both use present tense).
- Correct: John will read the paper then take a nap. He will sleep on the couch (both use future tense).

2. Stay consistent with plurality. Whichever form of plurality is used in the first part of a sentence or paragraph, use it throughout:

- Incorrect: A person (singular) should always have their (plural) passport.
- Correct: A person should always have a passport (both singular).
- Correct: A person should always have his or her passport (both singular).

- Correct: People should always have their passports (both plural).

- Incorrect: The team (singular) improved their (plural) average by 10%.
- Correct: The team improved its average by 10% (both singular).
- Correct: Players on the team improved their averages by 10% (both plural).

- Incorrect: A student (singular) should be able to choose their (plural) writing topics.
- Incorrect: Every student (singular) should be able to choose their (plural) writing topics.
- Correct: Students should be able to choose their writing topics (both plural).
- Correct: A student should be able to choose a writing topic (both singular).
- Correct: Each student should be able to choose his or her writing topic (both singular).

3. Double pronouns and noun-pronoun combinations should make sense when one is missing. A pronoun is a word that takes the place of a noun. For example, such personal pronouns as *I*, *me*, *you*, *him*, and *she* take the place of proper nouns or names. The following are some common pronouns:

COMMON PRONOUNS: anyone, anything, everyone, everything, he, her, him, himself, I, it, itself, me, myself, nothing, one, she, someone, something, them, themselves, they, us, we, who, you

To figure out the correct pronoun to use, read the sentence with each of the pronouns or pronoun-noun combinations separately. If the sentence makes sense, then you have the correct pronoun:

- Incorrect: Me and her will go to the store. (Me will go to the store. Her will go to the store.)
- Correct: She and I will go to the store. (She will go to the store. I will go to the store.)

- Incorrect: Lisa and her played golf. (Lisa played golf. Her played golf.)
- Incorrect: Her and Lisa played golf. (Her played golf. Lisa played golf.)
- Correct: Lisa and she played golf. (Lisa played golf. She played golf.)
- Correct: She and Lisa played golf. (She played golf. Lisa played golf.)

- Incorrect: The pie was eaten by he and I. (The pie was eaten by he. The pie was eaten by I.)
- Incorrect: The pie was eaten by him and I. (The pie was eaten by him. The pie was eaten by I.)
- Correct: The pie was eaten by him and me. (The pie was eaten by him. The pie was eaten by me.)

- Incorrect: Him and me painted the fence. (Him painted the fence. Me painted the fence.)

- Incorrect: Him and I painted the fence. (Him painted the fence. I painted the fence.)
- Correct: He and I painted the fence. (He painted the fence. I painted the fence.)

- Incorrect: The house was built by Mary and I. (The house was built by Mary. The house was built by I).
- Correct: The house was built by Mary and me. (The house was built by Mary. The house was built by me).

4. Use *that* for essential clauses and *which* for nonessential clauses. A *clause* is a part of a sentence that contains a subject (or noun) and a predicate (verb or action). An *essential clause* is one that is essential to the meaning of the sentence. That is, the meaning would change completely if the clause were removed. For an essential clause, the word *that* should be used without commas:

- Essential clause: The team that worked hard won the game.

This sentence indicates that (a) there is more than one team, (b) one team worked hard, (c) there are one or more other teams that did not work hard, and (d) of all the teams, it was the one that worked hard that won the game. This clause is therefore essential to the point of the sentence because we are clearly identifying a particular team.

A **nonessential clause** is like a theatrical aside. It adds dimension to the idea, but the meaning is still largely intact if the clause is not there. For a nonessential clause, the word *which* should be used along with a comma or commas:

- Nonessential clause: The team, which worked hard, won the game.
- Sentence without the clause: The team won the game.

In these sentences, the main idea is that the team won the game. They just happened to have worked hard. It does not indicate that there are other teams.

One way to help you remember: If the phrase *which by the way* could be inserted for *which* and the sentence still retains the desired effect, then use the word *which*. Use the word *that* to indicate *that particular one* when there is more than one choice:

- Essential Clause: The car that is blocking the driveway belongs to Bill. (Of all the cars, Bill's car is blocking the driveway. Here, there is an indication of more than one car.)
- Nonessential clause: The car, which is blocking the driveway, belongs to Bill. (The car, which by the way belongs to Bill, is blocking the driveway. Here, we do not know if there is more than one car.)

5. Use *that* and *which* for nonhuman entities and *who* or *whom* to indicate humans. As described earlier, commas should always be used to indicate nonessential clauses, whether *that*, *which*, or *who* is used:

- Incorrect essential clause: Those students that bought Andy's book received higher grades.
- Correct essential clause: Those students who bought Andy's book received higher grades.
- Correct nonessential clause: The stores, which sold Andy's book, earned more money.
- Correct essential clause: Those stores that sold Andy's book earned more money.

6. Use *who* if you can substitute *he* or *she* in the sentence; use *whom* if you can substitute *him* or *her* in the sentence. Hint: One way to remember this is to associate the *m* in *whom* with the *m* in *him*:

WHO = she or he

- Incorrect: The player whom you picked scored 27 points. (Her scored 27 points.)
- Correct: The player who you picked scored 27 points. (She scored 27 points.)

- Incorrect: Whom sang the song? (Her sang the song.)
- Correct: Who sang the song? (She sang the song.)

- Incorrect: Please describe the boy whom was at the event. (Him was at the event.)
- Correct: Please describe the boy who was at the event. (He was at the event.)

WHOM = her or him

- Incorrect: The person who I am referring to is missing. (I am referring to he.)
- Incorrect: The person to who I am referring is missing. (I am referring to he.)
- Correct: The person to whom I am referring is missing. (I am referring to him.)

- Incorrect: Bill talked to a clown who he met at the circus. (Bill talked to he.)
- Correct: Bill talked to a clown whom he met at the circus. (Bill talked to him.)

- Incorrect: Who did you give the cookies to? (Did you give the cookies to he?)
- Correct: To whom did you give the cookies? (Did you give the cookies to him?)

7. Do not end a sentence with a preposition. A preposition links a noun or pronoun to some other word in a sentence. You can remember what a preposition is by looking at the last eight letters of the word (*position*). A preposition tells the basic position of something (in, above, with, etc.). The following are some common prepositions:

COMMON PREPOSITIONS: about, above, across, after, against, along, among, at, before, behind, below, beside, between, but, by, despite, down, during, except, for, from, in, into, like, of, off, on, onto, out, over, past, since, through, to, toward, under, until, up, with, within, without

- Incorrect: Who are you going to the game with?
- Correct: With whom are you going to the game?

- Incorrect: In the paper, there were grammatical errors throughout.
- Correct: There were grammatical errors throughout the paper.

- Incorrect: Some common prepositions are found below.
- Correct: Below are some common prepositions.

- Incorrect: Time to come in.
- Correct: Time to come in the house.

8. Do Not Use Run-On Sentences. A run-on sentence is a sentence that goes on and on and on. It has at least two complete ideas (or independent clauses) but does not have the correct punctuation between the ideas. The following sentences contain two complete ideas: (a) Mary is strong, and (b) Mary can lift 150 pounds. The first sentence contains no punctuation, and the second uses the comma as a kind of pause mark. Both are incorrect:

- Correct: Mary is very strong she can lift 150 pounds.
- Correct: Mary is very strong, she can lift 150 pounds.

When sentences contain two or more complete ideas, use one of the following to separate the ideas: (a) a period to create two separate sentences, (b) a comma followed by a conjunction, or (c) a semicolon:

- Correct: Mary is very strong. She can lift 150 pounds.
- Correct: Mary is very strong, and she can life 150 pounds.
- Correct: Mary is very strong; she can lift 150 pounds.

A conjunction is a connecting word. It is used to connect two or more ideas in a sentence or between sentences. The following are some common conjunctions:

COMMON CONJUNCTIONS: after, although, and, as, because, before, but, except, if, like, nor, now, once, or, since, so, than, that, though, unless, until, when, where, whether, while

9. A Comparison Must Compare Something to Something Else. Comparison words indicate an entity or condition in relation to another entity or condition. Suffixes *-er* and *-est*, as well as *more* and *less*, are indicative of common comparison words. When using a comparison word, always make sure you are comparing something to something else:

- Incorrect: The new program helped students become better writers.

In this sentence, a comparison word is used (*better*) without a clear indication of what was being compared. The students became better writers but better than what or whom? Were they better than they were before the program? Were they better than another class? Or were they better than students who used another spelling program?

- Correct: The new program improved students' ability to write.
- Correct: The new program enabled students to write better than the old program.
- Correct: The new program was better than the old program in enabling students to write.

- Incorrect: The people who used this treatment were more likely to improve.
- Correct: The people who used this treatment were more likely to improve than those who did not use it.
- Correct: Most people who used this treatment showed improvement.

- Incorrect: There were more errors with the new program.
- Correct: There was an increase in errors with the new program.
- Correct: There were more errors with the new program than with the old program.
- Correct: There were more errors with the new program when compared to the old program.
- Correct: The new program resulted in increased errors.

- Incorrect: It is assumed that it will get better.
- Correct: It is assumed that it will improve.

Note: In our common conversations and nonacademic writing, we frequently use the comparative to indicate more or less of something.

THE LAST WORD

This chapter ends with three tips related to grammar and the writing process: First, focus on grammar primarily during the editing stage of your writing and not before. Concentrating too much at earlier stages will disrupt the academic writing process. Second, use the grammar-check function that comes with most word processor programs. While not always reliable, the grammar check will find most errors. They also provide grammar miniles-sons as you use them. However, they will not find all grammatical errors. And finally, find somebody to read your edited paper. When you have been working on a piece in the revision stages for a while, you tend to focus on ideas. It is very easy to miss simple grammatical and spelling errors. Everybody needs an editor.

Chapter Sixteen

Punctuation

Good academic writing communicates ideas efficiently and effectively.

Like grammar, correct punctuation also helps to create precision in writing. This chapter describes the basic punctuation information necessary to get you through most of your academic writing projects. You will notice that there is some overlap between punctuation and grammar. The punctuation information here should serve to reinforce some of the grammar information presented in the last chapter.

THE COMMA

A comma is used in the following situations.

1. To Separate Items in a Series. Use a comma to separate three or more items in a series. A comma should be inserted before the last conjunction (usually *and* or *or*) in the sentence:

- Example: In the forest there were lions, tigers, and bears.
- Example: Participants in the study were able to read, play tennis, sleep, or watch television.
- Example: To write well, you must read and take careful notes, use a predrafting strategy to generate ideas, and start your project early.

2. To Separate a Nonessential Clause. As described in the last chapter, a *clause* is a part of a sentence that contains a subject (or noun) and a predicate (verb or action). A nonessential clause is used like a theatrical aside or a "by the way" idea. The basic meaning of the sentence would still be intact without its inclusion. For example, the following sentence indicates the pie tasted stale. It just happened (by the way) to be made by Marvin:

99

- Nonessential clause: The pie, which was made by Marvin, tasted stale.
- Without the clause: The pie tasted stale.

The first sentence does not indicate that there are other pies, simply that the existing pie tasted stale. The fact that Marvin made the pie is an interesting aside but not an essential part of this sentence.

Conversely, an essential clause in the middle of a sentence is vital to the sentence and should not be separated by a comma. The following sentence tells us that there was more than one pie, but only the pie that was made by Marvin tasted stale. This is essential information, thus it is an essential clause. As described in the last chapter, *that* is used instead of *which*, and there are no commas:

- Essential clause: The pie that was made by Marvin tasted stale.

The following is another example of a sentence with a nonessential clause:

- Nonessential clause: The study, which was conducted in 1968, showed significant results.
- Without the clause: The study showed significant results.

This next sentence is also an example of a "by the way" clause. We are not comparing these students to other students. Instead, we are saying that they produced excellent papers, and by the way, they just happened to have started their projects early:

- Nonessential clause: The students, who started their projects early, produced excellent papers.
- Without the clause: The students produced excellent papers.

3. To Separate Two Independent Clauses in a Compound Sentence. A compound sentence is one that has two or more clauses, each of which makes sense by itself:

- Not a compound sentence: I will be working at home on Tuesday.
- Compound sentence: It is Tuesday, and I will be working at home.
- Clause 1: It is Tuesday.
- Clause 2: I will be working at home.

In the first sentence, *on Tuesday* is not a complete idea; however *It is Tuesday* is a complete idea. Use a comma followed by a conjunction to separate these ideas. The rule is this: If you have a compound sentence where both sides make sense as stand-alone sentences, then use a comma followed by a conjunction (*and*, *but*, *for*, *not*, *or*, *so*, or *yet*).

In the following sentence, both parts would work as complete sentences. A comma and conjunction is used to separate them:

- Compound sentence: The tests were completed, and the books were put away.
- Clause 1: The tests were completed.
- Clause 2: The books were put away.

Again, the following sentence shows that each clause is a separate idea and makes sense as stand-alone sentences:

- Two independent clauses: There were many games being played, but poker seemed to be preferred by most.
- Clause 1: There were many games being played.
- Clause 2: Poker seemed to be preferred by most.

In the first sentence, both clauses do not make sense as stand-alone sentences:

- Incorrect: John played professional baseball, and later played in a band.
- Complete idea: John played professional baseball.
- Not a complete idea: Later played in a band.
- Correct: John played professional baseball and later played in a band.

The insertion of the word *he* in the second part of that same sentence changes things because the clause now becomes a complete idea:

- Correct: John played professional baseball, and he later played in a band.
- Complete idea: John played professional baseball.
- Complete idea: He later played in a band.

4. After an Introductory Phrase. An introductory phrase sets up the next part of the sentence but does not make sense by itself. Use a comma to set this apart:

- After the test, John went home.
- Because it is Wednesday, the books were given to the students.
- As a result of the treatment, all participants showed improvement.
- If the apparatus works, then the test can continue.
- If you have a compound sentence where both sides make sense as stand-alone sentences, then use a comma followed by a conjunction.

THE SEMICOLON

A semicolon is used in the following situations.

1. To Separate Two Independent Clauses That Are Not Joined by a Conjunction. This means the semicolon takes the place of *and*, *but*, and *or*:

- No semicolon: The pie tasted great, but the ice cream was stale.
- Semicolon: The pie tasted great; the ice cream was stale.
- No semicolon: Writing is easy, and predrafting strategies are important.
- Semicolon: Writing is easy; predrafting strategies are important.

Each part of these sentences make sense by themselves: Writing is easy. Predrafting strategies are important. The conjunction is dropped and replaced with a semicolon.

2. To Separate a Series of Groups That Contain Commas Within One or More of the Groups. If I wanted to list three or more groups that contained three or more things in one or more of the groups, then commas would be used to separate the things within the groups, and semicolons would be used to separate the groups. This way the reader knows when the groups end and begin:

- Example: In this sentence, the first group is a, b, and c; the second group is d, e, f, and g; and the third group is h and i.

In the following sentence, there are two treatment groups and a control group:

- Example: In this study, the scores of the three groups were as follows: Treatment Group 1 averaged 80, 82, and 89; Treatment Group 2 averaged 75, 77, and 80; and the control group averaged 65, 68, and 69.

In the following sentence, the groups are the different dinner choices. As you can see in the first sentence, without the semicolon, there is chaos and confusion:

- Chaos and confusion: For dinner, you can have mangos, tacos, milk, and cheese, tomatoes, pancakes, and rice, or apples, toast, pop, and mustard.
- Correct: For dinner, you can have mangos, tacos, milk, and cheese; tomatoes, pancakes, and rice; or apples, toast, pop, and mustard.

3. To Indicate a Transitional Word or Phrase Between Two Related Independent Clauses. The technical name for this is a conjunctive adverb. You know them as connecting words or phrases. The most common of these are *however*, *therefore*, and *thus*. These are used to connect two related ideas:

- Common Conjunctive Adverbs: accordingly, also, as a result, besides, consequently, conversely, finally, further, furthermore, hence, however, indeed, instead, likewise, meanwhile, moreover, nevertheless, next, nonetheless, otherwise, on the other hand, similarly, still, subsequently, then, therefore, thus

Here, a semicolon is used in front of the connecting word or phrase and a comma behind it:

- Example: She may be small; however, she is very strong.
- Example: Academic writing is easy; however, it takes time and effort.

Reminder: An independent clause is one that makes sense by itself as a sentence. Each clause must be independent if a semicolon in front of the transition word is used.

- Correct: He read Andy's book carefully; thus, he was able to write effectively.
- Clause 1: He read Andy's book carefully.
- Clause 2: He was able to write effectively.

- Correct: He read Andy's book carefully; consequently, he wrote effectively.
- Correct: He read Andy's book carefully; subsequently, he wrote effectively.
- Correct: He read Andy's book carefully; as a result, he wrote effectively.
- Correct: He did not read Andy's book; nevertheless, he wrote effectively.
- Correct: He did not read Andy's book; still, he wrote effectively.

In each of these sentences, the second part of the sentence is directly related to the first part. This is what is meant by two related independent clauses. The following is an example of two independent clauses within a sentence that are unrelated:

- Two unrelated independent clauses: He will clean his sock drawer today, and then on Tuesday, he will shovel the snow.

THE COLON

The rule of thumb for the colon is that everything that follows the colon should be directly related to what preceded it. This is done two ways.

1. An Introductory Clause Followed by Information to Illustrate the Point. Here, the information before the colon tells what is coming after the colon:

- Example: There were two kinds of games: card games and board games.
- Example: There is one thing you must bring: a lifejacket.
- Example: The following section describes three types of writing: expository writing, persuasive writing, and inquiry writing.
- Example: There are six steps involved in the super-secret academic writing process: (a) researching to gather data, (b) predrafting, (c) the first draft, (d) revising, (e) editing, and (f) sharing.

2. An Introductory Clause Followed by a Complete Sentence That Illustrates the Point. In the following, the illustrating sentence that follows the colon is a complete sentence; thus, it begins with a capital letter:

- Example: All three agree: Buying Andy's book is important.
- Example: There is one important thing to remember: Always read and take careful notes.
- Example: The students all agree: Setting aside time to study is crucial to doing well in the course.
- Example: The one piece of advice given to first-year students is this: Start your papers early.

THE LAST WORD

This chapter describes how and when to use commas, semicolons, and colons. Two tips: First, just like grammar, focus on punctuation should occur primarily during the editing stage. And second, everybody needs an editor. You are not going to catch every punctuation error. Find somebody to read your edited paper.

Chapter Seventeen

Sentence Length

A frustrated or confused reader is soon a nonreader.

Do you think people will want to read your text if they have to struggle to figure out what you are trying to say?

LONG SENTENCES

Sentences that are too long will confuse the reader and make your writing less powerful. Keep in mind that short-term memory (STM) has a limited capacity. It can hold only about seven chunks of information for about 15 seconds. Read the following sentence:

- Too long: Despite a fairly substantial body of research related to effective writing instruction, as well as recommendations from a variety of different national literacy organizations, colleges and universities often implement writing programs for undergraduate students that go beyond preparing them for the next English course or that consist of more than assigning additional writing projects or requiring added writing-intensive courses; instead, they should implement well-structured programs with a coherent curriculum that is designed to teach students the specific processes related to academic writing as well as what the product should look like, and they should prepare students to do the types of writing and thinking that they will need to succeed in life outside the college or university setting.

This ubersentence contains 118 words. If you try to jam too many ideas into a single sentence, then it gets long and cumbersome. The reader has to try to hold onto the ideas at the beginning of the sentence while processing those found at the end. There are no natural pauses for processing. This clutters STM and creates frustration and confusion as the reader has to continually look back to see how one thing connects to another. In this example, the important ideas get lost in all the cumbersomeness.

SHORT SENTENCES

In academic writing, there is nothing wrong with a short sentence. However, too many short sentences will leave your writing sounding choppy and disjointed. The following 110 words are used to express the same ideas as those earlier; the difference is that each idea is put into its own sentence:

- Too short: There is abundant research about effective writing instruction. National literacy organizations have also made recommendations about effective writing instruction. Colleges and universities often fail to implement effective writing programs for undergraduate students. Effective writing programs do more than prepare students for the next English classes. These programs do not just assign more writing projects. They also do not simply require additional writing-intensive courses. Effective writing programs teach students the process related to academic writing. They also teach what the final product should look like. Effective writing programs prepare students to do the types of writing and thinking they will need to be successful outside the college or university setting.

JUST-RIGHT SENTENCES

It is best to mix the length of your sentences. The following paragraph is the result of many revisions. First, the topic sense is put at the beginning so the reader does not have to fish around for the main point. Next, ideas are moved around to create a smoother flow from one thing to the next. Finally, the wording and overall effect are examined. A few more words are need here (128), but the result is a paragraph that is easier to read and understand when compared to those previously:

- Just right: Most colleges and universities do not have programs in place to effectively teach undergraduate students how to write. In the design of these programs, a substantial body of research related to effective writing instruction often seems to be ignored. Also seemingly discounted are recommendations from national literacy organizations related to best practice in writing instruction. Effective college writing programs do not simply assign more writing projects within courses or require additional writing-intensive courses. Instead, effective college writing programs teach the process of writing as well as what the product should look like. These programs do more than prepare students for the next English class. Instead, they prepare students to do the types of writing and thinking they will need to succeed in life outside an academic setting.

The Process of Revising Paragraphs

The process for developing paragraphs with easy-to-read sentences is fairly straightforward: reread, review, revise, and repeat. Repeat the process several times. This is the only way to get the lumps out of your writing and create smooth, freely flowing sentences and paragraphs that read like melted butter. There is nothing magical about this. Repeat this process, looking for words that can be eliminated and connections that need to be inserted. Also, it is sometimes helpful to read sentences and paragraphs out loud. This will help to develop your writing ear.

A Citation Minilesson

Notice in the previous sample paragraph that some pretty audacious declarative statements are made. For example, "Most colleges and universities do not have programs in place to effectively teach undergraduate students how to write." The writer may think that this is the case, but in academic writing, you cannot just say something like this without some sort of supporting evidence. Declarative statements like this without any supporting evidence are called *I-think-isms*. I-think-isms in academic writing are bad. If a statement this bold and declarative is to be made, then an academic writer better have something to back it up. This is where we use reference citations.

Reference citations support the point you are trying to make. (Various types of research are described in Chapter 22.) They can be connected or tied to a single research study, review of research, research-based theory, theoretical articles, or books that have been peer-reviewed (see Chapter 2). The following paragraph shows how citations could be used to support the points I am trying to make:

> • Just right: Most colleges and universities do not have programs in place to effectively teach undergraduate students how to write (Smith, 2014). In the design of these programs, a substantial body of research related to effective writing instruction often seems to be ignored (Jones & Smith, 2012). Also seemingly discounted are recommendations from national literacy organizations related to best practice in writing instruction (Harrison, 2015). Effective college writing programs do not simply assign more writing projects within courses or require additional writing-intensive courses. Instead, effective college writing programs teach the process of writing as well as what the product should look like (Hanson, Smith, & Jones, 2013). These programs do more than prepare students for the next English class. Instead, they prepare students to do the types of writing and thinking they will need to succeed in life outside an academic setting (Smith, 2014).

A critical reader would then look at the list of references at the end of the paper to check the quality of the sources used. You should be extremely skeptical of generalized statements like this that are made without theoretical support or empirical evidence. For example, the writer's statement that most colleges and universities do not effectively teach undergraduate students how to write could be just his or her perception. Or, the writer could be making a generalization based on his or her own limited experience. Statements like this always need some sort of supporting evidence. The next chapter describes the use of references and citations in more depth.

THE LAST WORD

Remember, a frustrated or confused reader is soon a nonreader. It is of little use to be significant if nobody wants to read your work. Avoid long, cumbersome sentences. Also, reread your paragraphs many times to create smooth, flowing, concise sentences.

Chapter Eighteen

Citations

You are not a credible source.

Citing sources within your paper supports your ideas, sets your work in a theoretical context, and enhances the credibility of your writing. Citations also acknowledge the authors whose work you used and allow readers to examine your supporting documents.

To illustrate, read the following paragraph adopted from the book *10 Essential Instructional Elements for Students With Reading Difficulties: A Brain-Friendly Approach* (Johnson, 2016):

> During reading, information does not flow just one way from the page to the thalamus and up to the cortex. Brain imaging research shows that, as we process data taken in by the various senses, information also flows from the cortex down to the thalamus. As a matter of fact, there is almost 10 times more information flowing down from the cortex to the thalamus than up from the thalamus to the cortex. This means that higher structures of the brain (those involved in thought and reasoning) control or influence the lower structures during the act of processing visual information.

This paragraph is a fairly straightforward explanation of how things work. However, among some reading specialists, it is considered controversial because it challenges traditional paradigms. Here the writer is defining reading not simply as sounding out words but rather as creating meaning with print. In the following paragraph, the writer cites the sources used to support the declarative statements and enhance credibility:

During reading, information does not flow just one way from the page to the thalamus and up to the cortex (Gilbert & Sigman, 2007). Brain imaging research shows that, as we process data taken in by the various senses, information also flows from the cortex down to the thalamus (Engel, Fries, & Singer, 2001; Hawkins, 2004; Hruby, 2009; Koch, 2004). As a matter of fact, there is almost 10 times more information flowing down from the cortex to the thalamus than up from the thalamus to the cortex (Alitto & Usrey, 2003; Destexhe, 2000; Gilbert & Sigman, 2007; Koch, 2004; Sherman & Guillery, 2004; Strauss, 2011). This means that higher structures of the brain (those involved in thought and reasoning) control or influence the lower structures during the act of processing visual information (Ducket, 2008; Gilbert & Sigman, 2007; Hawkins, 2004).

Every source cited in the body of your work must appear in a list of references at the end of your text. This enables the reader to check the quality of these sources. As you can see in the following, the sources used to support the ideas here include primary research studies; reviews, analysis, and descriptions of research; and applications of research. These have all been published in peer-reviewed academic journals and books published by respected academic publishers. Also, these journals, authors, and publishers are all recognized within their various academic fields. In the list of sources, you will not see magazine or newspaper articles, Wikipedia websites, agenda-driven "research" conducted by think tanks or political groups, books published by nonacademic publishers, or studies conducted by for-profit entities:

References

Alitto, H. J., & Usrey, W. M. (2003). Corticothalamic feedback and sensory processing. *Current Opinion in Neurobiology, 13,* 440–445.

Destexhe, A. (2000). Modeling corticothalamic feedback and the gating of the thalamus by the cerebral cortex. *Journal of Physiology, 94,* 394–410.

Ducket, P. (2008). Seeing the story for the words: The eye movements of beginning readers. In A. Flurky, E. Paulson, & K. Goodman (Eds.), *Scientific realism in studies of reading* (pp. 113–128). New York: LEA.

Engel, A. K., Fries, P, & Singer, W. (2001). Dynamic predictions: Oscillations and synchrony in top-down processing. *Nature Reviews Neuroscience, 2,* 704–716.

Gilbert, C. S., & Sigman, M. (2007). Brain states: Top-down influence in sensory processing. *Neuron, 54,* 667–696.

Hawkins, J. (2004). *On intelligence.* New York: Henry Holt.

Hruby, G. G. (2009). Grounding reading comprehension in the neuroscience literatures. In S. E. Israel & G. P. Duffy (Eds.), *Handbook of research on reading comprehension* (pp. 189–223). New York: Routledge.

Koch, C. (2004). *The quest for consciousness: A neurobiological approach.* Englewood, CO: Roberts.

Sherman, S. M., & Guillery, R. W. (2004) The visual relays in the thalamus. In L. M. Chalupa & J. S. Werner (Eds.), *The visual neurosciences* (pp. 565–591). Cambridge, MA: MIT Press.

Strauss, S. L. (2011). Neuroscience and dyslexia. In A. McGill-Franzen & R. L. Allington (Eds.), *Handbook of reading disability research* (pp. 79–90). New York: Routledge.

CITING IN TEXT

Citing is different from quoting, which is described in Chapter 20. When citing, you must paraphrase the author's ideas in your own words. You cannot copy and use another author's phrases. This would be plagiarism (see Chapter 10).

One Author, One Article

To reference a work written by an author, make a declarative statement followed by the author's surname, a comma, and the year of publication in parentheses:

- Example: A recent study found that apples were better than oranges (Carson, 2016).
- Example: Apples are better than oranges (Carson, 2016).

If you included the author's name in your declarative statement, then put the year of publication of the article in parentheses directly following the name:

- Example: A study by Carson (2016) found that apples were better than oranges.

More Than One Author, One Article

To cite a work written by two authors, use the ampersand symbol (&) between the names when inside the parentheses, followed by a comma and the year of publication:

- Example: College students prefer apples over oranges (Woods & McDuffy, 2015).

To cite a work written by three or more authors, use a comma to separate the authors. Use an ampersand instead of the word *and* inside the parentheses:

- Example: Understanding the superiority of apples over oranges will enhance one's fruit selection (Carson, Fitzsimons, & Reuter, 2015).

More Than One Article

If many authors reach the same conclusion or make a similar point, then you can cite more than one work. In the following sentence, all the authors cited at the end of the sentence found that apples were better than oranges. Within the parentheses, the references are put in alphabetical order according to the lead author. A semicolon is used to separate each work:

- Example: Apples are better than oranges (Abbot, 2015; Carson, 2016; Costello, 2011; Everson, 2015; Fife & Taylor, 2010; Hardy & Laurel, 2010; Keaton & Marx, 2013; Perez, 2005).

Citing multiple sources like this really drives home the point that apples are indeed superior to oranges.

Three to Five Authors, One Article

For works written by three to five authors, the citation ends up sounding like a law firm. The first time you cite this in the text, you must list all the authors of the work with a comma between the last names:

- Example: A recent study found that the overuse of milk can lead to soggy breakfast cereal (Howard, Fine, & Howard, 2007).
- Example: Soggy breakfast cereal can be the result of overmilking (Howard, Fine, & Howard, 2007).

After you have made a full citation with three or more authors, you can use a shortcut with all subsequent citations of the same work. To do this, list the first author, followed by, *et al.* to replace the other names, followed by a comma and the year:

- Example: Most breakfast eaters prefer bananas on their soggy breakfast cereal (Howard et al., 2013).

Six or More Authors, One Article

Occasionally you will run across works that have six or more authors. To cite this within your work, include only the first name followed by *et al.* to replace all the other names. The only place that you would include all the names of all the authors would be in the full list of references at the end of the work:

- Incorrect: Apples are better than oranges (Howard, Keaton, Hardy, Marx, Laurel, Benny, & Fine, 2014).
- Correct: Apples are better than oranges (Howard et al., 2014).

- Incorrect: Howard, Keaton, Hardy, Marx, Laurel, Benny, and Fine (2014) found that mangos were better than peaches.
- Correct: Howard et al. (2014) found that mangos were better than peaches.

Citing by Mentioning the Author's Name

As described earlier, if you mention a single author's name within your work, then simply put the year in parentheses directly behind the name to cite it:

- Example: Carson (2016) recommends apples over oranges.

However, when referencing two or more authors' names within your text, use the whole word 'and' (instead of the ampersand), and put the year in parentheses directly behind the names to cite it:

- Example: Carson and Anderson (1991) found that asparagus was seldom used with breakfast cereal.

Rule of thumb: Use an ampersand inside the parentheses and *and* outside the parentheses.

A Stylistic Recommendation

This is a stylistic recommendation related to the use of citations: Do not let other voices dominate your work:

- Less effective: Reuter (2015) found that peach ice cream was dangerous. Jones and Smith (2012) reported that the consumption of peach ice cream often resulted in psychotic episodes. Keaton (2011) suggested that people who eat peach ice cream are much more likely to use hard drugs.

In this paragraph, we keep bumping into other authors. Whenever possible, simply state the idea in your own words and support it with a citation. This allows you to maintain a more powerful writing voice and creates a much smoother reading flow:

- More effective: Peach ice cream was found to be dangerous (Reuter, 2015). Consumption of peach ice cream has resulted in psychotic episodes (Jones & Smith, 2012) and led to hard drug use (Keaton, 2011).

Both of these paragraphs are technically correct; however, it can become distracting to read a paper filled with things other people have said, suggested, reported, or found. It is often more effective to simply say it and cite it. For example, in the following paragraph, we again keep bumping into other people. Stylistically, this reduces the flow and makes the writer seem like a timid little mouse:

- Less effective: Hanson (2015) says that eating apples is an important part of the writing process. Larson and Glockzin (2011) suggest that the consumption of apples my help to produce a more coherent paper. Perkins (2009) found that eating apples actually decreased the amount of time it took to write a paper. Fitzsimmons (2014) recommends eating apples as a cure for writer's block.

Instead, the following paragraph uses fewer words, and the reader does not have to stumble over a department store full of people to get your point. It also creates a more authoritative voice:

- More effective: Eating apples is an important part of the writing process (Hanson, 2015). They help to produce a more coherent paper (Larson & Glockzin, 2011) and decrease the amount of time spent writing (Perkins, 2009). Also, eating apples may help with writer's block (Fitzsimmons, 2014).

Again, both paragraphs are technically correct. However, the second one seems to flow a bit more easily than the other and gives the writer a more authoritative voice.

A Note About Alphabetical Order

As described earlier, when you list multiple citations for a single declarative statement, they should be put in alphabetical order as determined by the surname of the author or lead author of the work; for example, Barnes, 2015; Carson, 2009; Danielson & Anderson, 1999; Ernst, Ansel, Smithers, & Simpson, 2016. However, within a single work, you should never reorder the authors' names:

- Correct: Barnes, 2015; Carson, 2009; Danielson & Anderson, 1999; Ernst, Ansel, Smithers, & Simpson, 2016
- Incorrect: Anderson & Danielson, 1999; Ansel, Ernst, Simpson, & Smithers, 2016; Barnes, 2015; Carson, 2009

Why? The order of names in a work is usually determined by the degree of the contribution made by each author. There is much more prestige being the lead author of a work than there is being listed later down the list. Thus, if you start rearranging the order of names within a specific citation, then you will have some very upset lead authors.

A COMMON QUESTION

Do you need to cite every single sentence in your work that contains an idea that did not come directly from your head? No. That would look silly and make it much harder to read:

- Do not do this: As consumers of scientific inquiry related to education, we must be aware of the differences between science and *pseudoscience* (Smith, 2015). Science uses perceived reality to determine beliefs (Smith, 2015). That is, data are collected to determine what is believed (Smith, 2015). Pseudoscience uses beliefs to determine perceived reality (Smith, 2015). One starts with a strong belief and then looks for data to support that belief (Smith, 2015). Pseudoscience is often used by companies, groups, or individuals to demonstrate that their product, method, or ideology is the most effective or best (Smith, 2015). Often education decisions are made based on pseudoscience (Smith, 2015). Science provides an honest analysis of the situation and is much preferred to pseudoscience (Smith, 2015).

Remember, we cite to give proper credit to the authors whose work we are using, to support or give credence to our ideas, and to set our thoughts in a theoretical context. Once you acknowledge from where the idea came, you can explain and develop the author's ideas. The only caveat here is that you must paraphrase the idea using your own words. In the following paragraph, it is generally assumed that these are all Smith's (2015) ideas:

- Instead, do this: As consumers of scientific inquiry related to education, we must be aware of the differences between science and *pseudoscience* (Smith, 2015). Science uses perceived reality to determine beliefs. That is, data are collected to determine what is believed. Pseudoscience uses beliefs to determine perceived reality. One starts with a strong belief and then looks for data to support that belief. Pseudoscience is often used by companies, groups, or individuals to demonstrate that their product, method, or ideology is the most effective or best. Often education decisions are made based on pseudoscience. Science provides an honest analysis of the situation and is much preferred to pseudoscience.

In the following paragraph, there are some ideas by Jones (2015) separated by an idea by Dyson (2009). To reintroduce a Jones idea, it is cited a second time within the same paragraph. Are there hard and fast rules related to this? No. Again, citing is used here to lend credibility to declarative statements. Because the writer is not a recognized expert in this area, citing others increases the likelihood that the declarative sentences included in this work will have some degree of credence:

- Example: Scientific knowledge is a body of knowledge generated by research. *Research* is a way of seeing, a procedure used to view and re-view the world in order to understand it (Jones, 2015). Research is the systematic method used to collect data to answer questions (Dyson, 2009). The systematic method used by the researcher is the lens through which the world is viewed. Different research methods or lenses provide different views of reality. A variety of scientific methods are used to study the unknown (Jones, 2015); however, these methods tend to be put into two broad categories: quantitative and qualitative.

THE LAST WORD

Unless you are a world-renowned expert, you are not a credible source. In academic writing, citations are used to support your ideas and lend credibility to your writing.

Chapter Nineteen

The Reference List

The reference list is a quick and easy way to evaluate the sources used for a book or article. Beware any academic document that does not cite its sources or include a reference list.

The reference list is found at the end of your work. It contains the full references of all articles that are cited in the body of your work. These are listed in alphabetical order by the authors' surnames. Everything cited or quoted in the body of your text must appear here. Likewise, you may not put any citations on the reference page that do not appear in the body of your text. Those are the rules.

The following references are described using APA style. Hanging indentations are used on the reference page. That means that you start the citation flush left. If the reference flows into the next line, then this next line should be indented five spaces. There are no extra spaces between citations. (You should be using double spacing throughout your paper.)

The following sections describe what full references should look like.

PERIODICALS

Journal Articles With One Author

A reference for a journal article contains the following: (a) the author's surname, a comma, initials separated with spaces, and a period; (b) the year the article was published in parentheses followed by a period; (c) the name of the journal article, capitalizing only the first letter of the first word in the title, followed by a period; (d) the name of the journal, with the major words capitalized and in italics, followed by a comma; (e) the volume number and a comma with continued italics; and (f) the page range, using an en dash, on which the article is found followed by a period:

Author, A. A. (2016). Name of the article. *Name of the Journal, 32,* 34–41.
Brady, T. (2011). The art and science of academic writing. *Journal of Higher Education, 26,* 89–95.
Carson, J. (2015). How to write successful academic papers and journal articles. *Writing Digest, 3,* 123–129.

Journal Articles With a Subtitle

The first word in the title of a journal article is capitalized, followed by a colon and subtitle. The first word following the full colon is also capitalized:

Johnson, A. (2016). The key to writing well: Taking careful notes. *The Journal of Writing, 57*(4), 234–301.
Rodgers, A. (2015). The referenced page: Indenting is important. *Academic Writing Quarterly, 34,* 87–90.
Shakespeare, W. (2016). Writing successfully: Reading a lot and revising often. *The International Journal of Academic Writing, 57,* 34–55.

Journal Articles With More Than One Author

Articles with more than one author are the same as with one author except that the authors' surnames and initials are separated with commas:

Johnson, A., Bridgewater, T., & Ponder, C. (2016). The magic of paragraphs. *The Journal of Writing Research, 57,* 122–131.

Journal Articles That Are Also Published Online

Articles found online or those published in a print version that are also published online often have a digital object identifier (DOI). This is used to provide a permanent link to the article's location on the Internet. Simply include the DOI at the end, with no ending period:

Luther, L. (2016). Reference citations for academic articles. *Journal of Writing and Research, 72,* 335–340. doi: 10.1036/0268-6234.34.5.225

Online Journal Articles Without a DOI

For online journal articles that do not have a DOI, include *Retrieved from* followed by the URL right after the name of the journal, with no ending period:

Manning, P. (2016). The importance of process. *Writing Research Quarterly, 37.* Retrieved from http://www.wrq.psu.edu/wrq/iop.html

An Article Found in a Magazine

As discussed earlier, magazine articles are not good sources to use in an academic article. Use them sparingly:

Marino, D. (2015, July 16). Magazine articles are not good sources for academic writing. *Newsweek*, 39–42.

A Newspaper Article

Newspaper articles are also not good sources to use in academic writing. Be equally spare in their use:

Favre, B. (2015, September 5). Newspaper articles are not good sources for academic writing. *The New York Post*, p. A11.

BOOKS

Books With One Author

A citation from a book is similar to that of a journal article. It contains the following: (a) the author's surname, a comma, initials, and a period; (b) year of publication in parentheses followed by a period; (c) the name of the book italicized, capitalizing only the first letter, followed by a period; (d) the place in which it was published, and (e) the publisher, removing unnecessary words like *Publisher*, *Co.*, and *Inc*.

Author, A. (2016). *Name of the book*. City, State: Publisher.
Rivers, P. (2015). *Revising your academic writing*. Newburg, MA: Ellen & Baycon.

Books With a Subtitle

Just as with a journal article, the subtitle follows a colon, and the first letter of the first word directly following a full colon is capitalized:

Johnson, A. (2016). *Academic writing: Process and product*. Lanham, MD: Rowman & Littlefield.

Books With Many Authors

Just as with journal articles, include a comma between the authors and use ampersand instead of the word *and*.

Johnson, A., Leno, J., Carson, J., & Stewart, J. (2015). *The best writing book ever published*. Newburg, MA: Ellen & Baycon.

Books of a Later Edition

A book published may be the third or fourth editions of one written earlier. This tells the reader that the book was so popular that it was updated and later editions were printed. Here, *4th ed.* is in parentheses to indicate fourth edition. The *ed* is in lowercase with a period after it. A period also follows the last parenthesis:

Johnson, A. (2012). *A short guide to action research* (4th ed.). Boston, MA: Allyn and Bacon.

An Online Book

The citation for an online book is exactly the same as a printed version except that you include *Retrieved from* followed by the URL right after the title, with no final period:

Johnson, A. (2014). *Phonics instruction and word identification skills.* Retrieved from http://www. amazon.com/Phonics-Word-Identification-Skills-Strategies-ebook/dp/B00IYWA4JI

An Edited Book

An edited book is one in which one or more people have edited the writings of other authors and compiled them in a single book. This is identified by including *Ed.* for one editor or *Eds.* for more than one editor in parentheses. *Ed.* starts with a capital letter so that the reader is able to quickly make the distinction between edition and editor:

Editor, A. (Ed.). (2016). *Title of the book in italics.* City, State: Publisher.

In the first citation here, we can assume that editor Jameson has put together a book where several different writers are describing their craft. In the second citation, editors Kent and White have put together a selection of writers, each of whom has one or more chapters that are somehow related to note-taking and academic writing:

Jameson, J. (Ed.). (2016). *Writers and their craft.* Minneapolis: Peersin.
Kent, J., & White, P. (Eds.). (2016). *The importance of careful note-taking on the academic writing in 21st century.* New York: McGoo-Hall.

Note: The ampersand is used between the surnames of multiple editors in the reference list instead of the word *and*.

A Chapter in an Edited Book With One Editor

To cite the work of one author of a chapter in an edited book, the following information is listed in this order: (a) the surname of the author of the chapter, followed by a comma and initials separated by spaces; (b) year of publication; (c) the title of the chapter with first word capitalized; (d) *In* followed by the editor or editors (initials before the surname); (e) *Ed.* or *Eds.* in parentheses followed by a comma; (f) the book title in italics; (g) *pp.* and the page range in which the chapter is found in parentheses followed by a period, and (h) the publishing information (location, full colon, and publisher):

Author, A. (2016). Title of chapter. In E. Editor (Ed.), *Title of book in italics* (pp. 27–39). City, State: Publisher.

Lane, L., & Olson, J. (2016). The importance of accurate citations. In G. Taylor (Ed.), *Writers and their craft* (pp. 57–84). New York: McGoo-Hall.

A Chapter in an Edited Book With More Than One Editor

The only difference between this citation and the previous one is that you would include *Eds.* instead of *Ed.*:

Parr, J. (2015). Using the objective stance in academic writing. In. J. Jameson & P. White (Eds.), *Writing for success* (pp. 121–149). New York: McGoo-Hall.

THE LAST WORD

You will refer back to this page often. You may wish to put a Post-it note here. If you need to cite something that was not included here, then do an Internet search using the terms "APA citation" or "MLA citation," and include whatever it is that you need to cite.

Chapter Twenty

Quotations

Effective academic writing can be read with minimal effort.

Quotations in academic writing are used for a variety of purposes: They can provide a fresh perspective or voice in your academic writing. They can be used to highlight a particular point. Quotes are also used when a particular writer may have said something so absolutely perfectly that paraphrasing will simply not do. Also, quoting a well-known expert in the field can sometimes be used to add credence to your ideas. Finally, quotes are used when referring to a specific rule, law, statute, standard, or some other document or text where the exact wording is important. However, as noted here, quotations should be used sparingly.

QUOTATION GUIDELINES

Material quoted from another author's work must be reproduced exactly and cited within the text. You cannot copy phrases or sentences that somebody else has written and lead readers to think that they are yours. This is a form of plagiarism (see Chapter 10). A variety of quoting options are described and illustrated here.

Short Quotes Without Mentioning the Author

To state exactly what an author has written without mentioning that author's name within the sentence, enclose the author's exact words in quotation marks. This is followed by the author's last name, year of publication, and page number all in parentheses and separated by commas. A period is placed outside the parentheses:

- Example 1: "For fewer than 40 words, put the quote right in the paragraph" (Author, 2016, p. 123).
- Example 2: College campuses seem to be recognizing the importance of the writing process. "Most college writing instructors now teach the process related to academic writing and not just what the finished product should look like" (Taylor, 2016, p. 125).
- Example 3: College campuses are places where students are exposed to a diversity of views. "They are a melting pot of views and experiences, a great finger painting upon which ideas are pushed around, tested, and combined with unique effects" (Fife, 2015, p. 125). These diverse views provide rich opportunities for students to identify and develop their own new values and belief systems.

Inserting Quoted Material Into the Middle of a Sentence

To insert a quote in the middle of a sentence, list the author, year, and page number separated by commas and directly behind the quoted material. This is often done if you want to use a snappy phrase that somebody else has written:

> Because the federal report stated that "college students generally write like monkeys" (Davis, 2015, p. 115), many universities have begun formal instruction related to the writing process during their writing courses.

Short Quotes That Mention the Author

To state exactly what an author said and mention this name within the sentence, put the year of publication in parentheses behind the author's name and put the page number in parentheses behind the quote followed by a period:

- Sanchez (2015) stated that "most first-year college students have no idea how to approach academic writing" (p. 125).

Block Quotations

Block quotations are used if you have 40 or more words to quote. Here the quotation marks are omitted. Instead, you start a new line and indent the entire quotation five spaces. If you need to quote two or more paragraphs, then new paragraphs are indented an additional five spaces. The parenthetical citation information appears at the end of the block quotation but outside the final period. Block quotations should use the same spacing as the rest of your paper:

Educational research is a key factor in enabling school administrators, principals, teachers, and parents to make sound decisions. Teachers and schools have a tremendous effect on student learning and achievement. This effect is more likely to be positive if the decisions related to policy, curriculum, and teaching practices are made based on what a body of research has determined to be best practice. Unfortunately, this is not always the case.

Educational decisions are often made based on personal experience. A teacher may have tried a strategy or approach or had a particular experience, and this becomes the basis of all future decisions. This is called anecdotal evidence, and while it is very powerful (because of the personal connection), it is not a very sound approach to use for decision-making. (Garbanzo, 2015, p. 146)

Quotations That Span More Than One Page

Occasionally, you may be quoting something that spans more than one page. Instead of *p.*, use *pp.* to indicate page numbers:

Educational research is used to create the theories upon which we design educational policies and practices. Theories help to organize relevant empirical facts (empirical means they can be observed or measured) in order to create a context for understanding phenomena. Sometimes people try to dismiss an idea or practice with which they do not agree by saying it is just a bunch of theory, meaning I guess that the theoretical realm is somehow far removed from the practical realm, perhaps even having a different set of laws that govern it. But this would be a misunderstanding of what a theory is.

A theory is a way to explain a set of facts. Put another way, if reality were a dot-to-dot picture, then a theory would be a way to connect a set of data dots. However, varying theories connect different data dots in different ways, resulting in a wide variety of pictures and practices. Thus, varying theoretical perspectives, while based on a set of empirical data, can often advocate different practices or practical notions. An example would be behavioral learning theory and cognitive learning theory, both of which are based on solid empirical evidence. (Smith, 2016, pp. 32–33)

ANOTHER WORD OF WARNING

Just like citations, quotations should be used sparingly. You give away your authority if you allow your writing to become a series of "he said, she said":

• Writing that lacks authority: Jones (1998) believes that "choice is the American way" (p. 134). Smith (1981) said that "Freedom is the heart of our democracy" (p. 112). Frankel (1965) states,
Freedom and choice are an integral part of what makes up our nation. We must believe in people's ability to make good choices. Without this belief, our government becomes a controlling parent figure. However, with freedom and choice comes responsibility. The question then becomes, How do we make sure that our students

are able to make responsible choices? The answer is, by giving them instruction in and practice with making choices. (p. 456)

Using citations is usually more efficient and effective than using quotes:

> • Writing with authority: Choice is part of American culture (Jones, 1998) and an integral part of our democracy (Frankel, 1965; Smith, 1981). Providing instruction in choice-making and allowing students opportunities to practice this skill will make them better able to make good choices in the future (Frankel, 1965).

Again, this is one of those stylistic matters. Both of these paragraphs are technically correct. The second one is more concise and easier to read and creates a paper that does not feel like a regurgitation of what a bunch of people said or wrote.

THE LAST WORD

Quotes are to be used sparingly. They should not be used to make your salient points or arguments but rather to support them. Also, quotes should not be used to carry your content but to illustrate your content. Just as with citations, the full reference for any quoted material must be listed in alphabetical order on the reference page. This allows the reader to identify your source.

Chapter Twenty-One

Quantitative Data, Tables, Figures, and Graphs

Using too many words can cover up your ideas.

When do you use numerals, and when do you use words to express arithmetic concepts?

USING NUMERALS

Use numerals to express arithmetic concepts with the following:

- **Numbers 10 and above:** There were 42 different incidents that occurred this year.
- **Dates:** This study took place on January 15, 2016.
- **Ages:** At the beginning of this study, the boy was 5 years old.
- **Time:** Participants in this study began recording their observations at 1:00 p.m. They continued for 2 hours and 9 minutes.
- **People in a study:** This observational study included 15 participants: 9 males and 8 females.
- **Grade level:** Beginning in grade 5, children read more expository text than narrative text. (Note: It is *grade 5* but *fifth grade*.)
- **Chapters:** All reported that Chapter 22 was the most compelling chapter of the book.
- **Pages:** Page 9 of this text included a fascinating description of how to determine appropriate academic sources.
- **Scales or rating systems:** She scored a 6 on a 10-point scale.
- **Money:** Subjects in this study were paid $6 for participating in the survey.

- **Numbers below 10 grouped for comparison with other numbers 10 and above:** In this study, 9 out of 12 participants showed significant improvement.

USING WORDS

Use words to express arithmetic concepts with the following:

- **Numbers below 10:** She answered four out of seven questions incorrectly.
- **Numbers that begin a title:** Ms. Swanson read the book *Three Tidy Tigers* to her first-grade class.
- **Numbers that begin a sentence:** Twelve children fell asleep during the story. (However, try to avoid starting sentences with numbers.)
- **Common fractions:** Two thirds of the participants in the study reported a problem with implementation.

REPORTING NUMBERS

There are four rules for reporting numbers.

1. Numbers Should Be Reported in Descending Order (From Greatest to Least).

- Example: Of the people interviewed for this study, 27 were diagnosed with depressive disorders, 26 with anxiety disorders, 8 with neurocognitive disorders, and 2 with obsessive-compulsive disorders.

In this example, the writer begins using numerals instead of words (27 with depressive disorders); therefore, the writer had to remain consistent even though some numbers were below 10 (8 with neurocognitive disorders and 2 with obsessive-compulsive disorders).

2. Tell What You Are Observing First.

- Example: This study was designed to determine the types of movie genres that were popular among college students. Out of 133 total responses . . .

3. Report the Total Number Before You Report Categories. Both of the following examples are correct; however, the second seems a less repetitive:

- Example 1: Out of 133 total responses, 51 preferred action/thriller, 41 preferred comedies, 34 preferred romance/relationship, and 7 preferred science fiction movies.
- Example 2: Out of 133 total responses, the following preferences were noted: 51 action/thriller, 41 comedies, 34 romance/relationship, and 7 science fiction.

4. Stay Consistent With the Order of Gender or Other Categories. Report numbers in descending order; however, when reporting such categories as gender, the order of the first example must remain consistent throughout:

- Example: There were 31 students in the survey: 16 males and 15 females. Nine males and 7 females were Caucasian, 5 males and 6 females were Black, and 2 males and 2 females were Asian.

In this example, the writer started with the largest total category (Caucasian). The order with this category was 9 males and 7 females. In the following categories (Black and Asian), even though the numbers of females were greater than or equal to the numbers of males, they were reported second so as to stay in a consistent order.

TABLES

Tables are a very efficient and visual way to organize and report data. They are especially useful if you have a great deal of numerical data to report. For example, in a study conducted to determine why college students consume energy drinks, I could present the data in paragraph form:

A study was conducted to determine the factors that drive college students to consume energy drinks. Out of 550 students surveyed, 226 were females, and 224 were males. The primary reasons stated for consuming energy drinks were as follows: 25% of the males and 24% of the females stated energy boost, 20% of the males and 17% of the females stated taste, 14% of the males and 5% of the females stated to stay awake while drinking, 11% of the males and 23% of the females stated mental alertness, 10% of the males and 10% of the females stated to drink more alcohol, 10% of the males and 1% of the females stated athletic performance, 8% of the males and 14% of the females stated to enhance studying, 1% of the males and 3% of the females stated to reduce hangovers, and 1% of the males and 3% of the females stated to hide the flavor of alcohol.

This paragraph is certainly correct; however, it's not easy to digest this amount of information. Table 21.1 is used to report the same information. For each gender, the preference is listed from greatest to least.

Parentheses should be used to refer to a table in the text (see Table 21.1). Because it is a title, *Table* is capitalized. The table number should be listed above the table, flush left. The title should be italicized and listed on the next line, also flush left, capitalizing the first letter of principle words. This lets the reader know quickly and easily exactly what is being read.

If you are using chapters, then break the table and figure numbers into chapters. Table 21.1 means Chapter 21, Table 1. If you are writing a non-chaptered text, then simply label tables and figures in their order of their reference in the text; for example, Figure 1, Figure 2, Table 1, Table 2, and so on.

In Table 21.2, the same data are reported; however, the data here are grouped and listed in descending order according to factor totals. (Note: Because Table 21.2 is referenced in the sentence, it was not necessary to put *see Table 21.2* in parentheses.)

One final thing to note before concluding this section: Data presented in tables are meant to replace information written in the text. Thus, in your text, you might refer to the data, but do not duplicate table information in the text. In other words, data can be presented in paragraph form or table form but not both. And because tables make data readily available to the reader in a very consumable form, this will usually be the preferred form.

FIGURES

Figures include lists, graphs, diagrams, or pictures. Figures are labeled differently from tables. The figure number is italicized, flush left, and followed by a period. The title of the figure follows and is not italicized. In the title, only the first letter is capitalized, and the last word is followed by a period (see Figure 21.1). Figures are not the same as tables and should be labeled and

Table 21.1
Factors for College Students' Consumption of Energy Drinks

Males	Females
Energy boost - 25%	Energy boost - 24%
Taste - 20%	Mental alertness - 23%
Stay awake while drinking - 14%	Taste - 17%
Mental alertness - 11%	Enhance studying - 14%
Drink more alcohol - 10%	Drink more alcohol - 10%
Athletic performance - 10%	Hide flavor of alcohol - 5%
Enhance studying - 8%	Stay awake while drinking - 5%
Reduce hangover - 1%	Reduce hangover - 3%
Hide flavor of alcohol -1%	Athletic performance - 1%

Table 21.2

Factors for College Students' Consumption of Energy Drinks

Factor	Male	Female	Total
Energy Boost	25%	24%	49%
Taste	20%	17%	37%
Mental alertness	11%	23%	34%
Enhance studying	8%	14%	22%
Drink more alcohol	10%	10%	20%
Stay awake while drinking	14%	5%	19%
Athletic performance	10%	1%	11%
Hide flavor of alcohol	1%	5%	6%
Reduce hangover	1%	3%	4%

counted differently. For example, I have used two tables thus far in this chapter, but this is the first figure, so it is labeled *Figure 21.1.*

Graphs

Graphs are listed as figures. Bar graphs are used to show comparisons (see Figure 21.2). Line graphs are used to show change over time (see Figure 21.3).

Other

Pictures, photographs, maps, illustrations, or sample products are all examples of figures and should be referred to in the same way as the figures described previously. If you have an abundance of figures, then they should be included in an appendix at the end of your report and simply referred to in the body of your text.

Figure 21.1. The academic writing process.

1. Research to gather data. Usually this means finding sources, reading and taking careful notes. However, data can also be collected other ways.
2. Pre-drafting. As the name implies, this is what is done before writing the first draft. This involves things such as planning, creating outlines, talking with others, generating ideas, or finding structure.
3. First-draft. This is the first attempt to get ideas on the page.
4. Revise. This is the heart of the writing process. Here the writer rereads, reshapes, gets feedback, and revises many times.
5. Editing. Editing should occur only after a piece has been revised several times. Here the writer looks for spelling, punctuation, and grammatical errors.
6. Share. This is the very last step. This is where the paper is sent out into the world.

Figure 21.2. Beverage preference of college students.

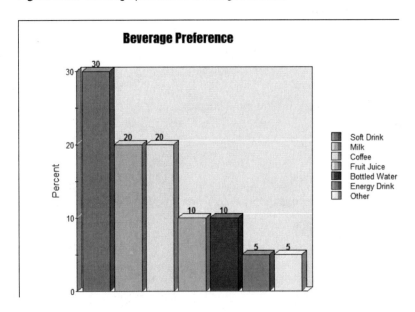

Figure 21.3. Weekly study hours.

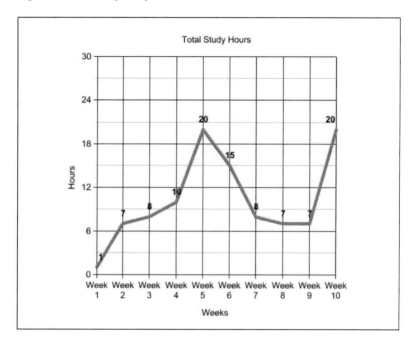

IV

Using Research in Academic Writing

Chapter Twenty-Two

The Basics Elements of Research

Research is a way of seeing. *Research*, or *re-search*, means to search again to re-view things in different ways.

It is beyond the scope of this book to delve deeply into various research methods. Instead, the following are some basic concepts related to research and research methodology. Depending on the field or area of your academic writing, you will often be asked to use research to support your views. Understanding these basic elements of research will enable you to do this.

RESEARCH

Research is the process of asking questions and using data to answer these questions (Johnson, 2012). Data are collected using some type of objective, systematic procedure called a scientific method. There are a variety of scientific methods used to study phenomena; however, these methods tend to be put into two broad categories: experimental research and descriptive research.

Experimental Research

Experimental research is what most people associate with research. Here, the researcher sets up an observation or experiment to figure out what the effect of one thing (independent variable) might be on other (dependent variable). In order to make an accurate prediction or causal connection, the researcher creates an artificial environment that isolates a particular variable by controlling all the extraneous variables. That is, everything is the same in two or more groups or situations except the thing about which the researcher wishes to investigate. This enables a comparison to be made (usually one thing to another or before and after).

The following are some important terms in understanding experimental research:

- The *independent variable* is the approach, treatment, or element that the researcher manipulates or isolates to determine a possible effect. It's what is done or not done to people, animals, plants, or things in order to determine a possible effect.
- The *dependent variable* is the result or the effect that the independent variable has. It's usually what is measured, recorded, or observed. An easy way to remember the distinction between these two variables is to think of the dependent variable as depending on the treatment or independent variable.
- The *treatment group*, or experimental group, is the group of subjects, participants, entities, or objects that are exposed to the independent variable.
- The *control group* is a group as similar as possible in all characteristics to the treatment group; however, this group is not exposed to the independent variable so that a comparison can be made.
- A *random grouping* in an experimental study is the random or unsystematic assignment of subjects to either the treatment or control group. In order to be a true experiment, there must be a randomized assignment to groups.
- The *quasi-experimental method* is experimental research without randomized groupings. In education and other social sciences, random assignment to groups is often not possible because of ethical reasons. (For example, you cannot withhold treatment to one group simply to study its effects.) Thus, in education and other social sciences, the quasi-experimental method is most often used where you study groups already in existence (such as classrooms).
- The *research question* is the specific question the researcher is trying to answer.
- The *hypothesis* is a tentative statement that can be supported if the outcome of the experimentation is as expected. That is, we speculate the possible cause-and-effect relationship between our independent and dependent variables.
- A *theory* is an interrelated set of facts or concepts that are used to explain a body of data.

One of the problems with the controlled environments used in experimental research in the social sciences is that they are not real. That is, manipulating conditions in order to isolate a variable creates an artificial environment. Thus, you end up studying something that may not replicate reality. For example, the way a person might react to an independent variable in the controlled space of a laboratory setting could be much different than how that person might react when confronted with the same variable in a real-life setting. This is not to say that experimental research in the social sciences does not provide important and useful data. What it means is that experimental research in the social sciences provides just one part of a total picture.

Descriptive Research

Descriptive research examines and describes the world as it is (Fraenkel & Wallen, 2003). It looks at existing numbers, groups, or conditions without manipulating them. Three types of descriptive research are described here: correlational research, causal-comparative research, and qualitative research.

Correlational Research

Correlational research uses statistical procedures to determine whether and to what degree two things are related. For example, there is a strong correlation (or co-relation) between income and student achievement. As parents' income rises, so too do scores on their children's standardized achievement tests (Sirin, 2005). As parent income decreases, so too do student scores. An increase or decrease in one thing seems to be related to a similar increase or decrease in another thing. This is called a positive correlation. A negative correlation is when an increase in one thing seems to be related to a decrease in another. For example, an increase in the number of free and reduced lunches at a school is strongly correlated with a decrease in student achievement at that school as measured by scores on standardized achievement tests (NAEP, 2014).

A word of warning here: Correlation does not infer causation. Just because two variables are co-related, we cannot say that one causes the other. There may be other variables at play. In the previous example, free and reduced lunches are related to lower achievement test scores, but we cannot say that they caused achievement test scores to go down. It is highly doubtful that the act of giving food to students at a free or reduced cost causes impairment to their cognitive functioning. Instead, free and reduced lunch is an indication of another variable (poverty), which is often associated with increases of chronic and acute stressors, such as high rates of crime and violence, poor health care and nutrition, a lack of good books, fewer computers, and fewer enrichment experiences. These are all factors common to children living in poverty that have been shown to be related to a decrease in school performance (Jensen, 2009).

Causal-Comparative Research

Causal-comparative research compares groups or entities in order to identify causal relationships between variables or look for differences occurring over time. For example, Dr. Jones wanted to investigate the effectiveness of a new approach to reduce prison recidivism. To do this, she had to examine the recidivism rates of all the prisons using the new approach. She compared these to prisons using other approaches and prisons that used no approaches. The independent variable here would be the approach used; the dependent variable would be the rates of recidivism. If the recidivism rates for the new approach were lower than the others and the differences were statistically significant, then it would be reasonable to assume that this new approach might hold promise.

No research method is perfect. One of the issues with causal-comparative research is that all the variables are not controlled. For example, we do not know if prisons and prisoners in Wisconsin are the same as prisons and prisoners in Texas. We also do not know how and to what degree the various approaches to recidivism were implemented in each case. One of the ways to try to circumvent this is through large sample sizes. Another way is to use matched samples. For every type of prison and prisoner in one group, we put a similar type of prison and prisoner in the other group. Again, every type of research has strengths and limitations.

Qualitative Research

Qualitative research (sometimes called naturalistic inquiry) uses systematic observations in order to understand a phenomenon, condition, or situation. Examples of qualitative research include Jean Piaget's study of children's thinking and learning, Jane Goodall's study of chimpanzees in the jungle, or Charles Darwin's observations of the origins of species on the Galapagos Islands. Examples of data collection in a qualitative research might include interviews, structured observations, surveys, checklists, samples of dialogue, audio or video recordings, records, artifacts, case studies, products, performances, or field notes.

One example of qualitative research is Shirley Brice Heath's groundbreaking ethnography *Ways With Words* (1983). She spent 10 years interacting with three different communities in the Piedmont region of the Carolinas from 1969 to 1978. The students she studied were the first to move from their isolated community schools into a common integrated school in the early days of desegregation. In this classic study, she came to understand how language learning at home and in a community can affect school success and achievement.

THE LAST WORD

So which research method is the best? Different kinds of questions call for different kinds of research design. There is no such thing as the "best" research method. However, the following are four important ideas to keep in mind when evaluating research for use in academic writing.

1. Research Is Not Research Unless and Until There Has Been a Blind Peer Review.

Conducting a study or collecting data can be used to inform individual practice in whatever field or practice you are in, but these should not be considered research in the larger sense. For example, a for-profit company may conduct a study that finds (surprisingly enough) that their product or service is effective. This is all well and good, but if they use their study to say "Research shows that Product X is effective," then this would be a misleading. Also, a political group or think tank may collect data to support a particular position, but without a peer review, we do not know if their question-asking, data selection and collection, and interpretation of the data were objective. They could reasonably say, "The data we collected show that . . ." but in an academic sense of the term, it would be inaccurate and misleading to say "Research shows that . . ." When you get your own talk radio show, you can say whatever you want, but in academic writing, you must make this distinction.

Once a study has been conducted, real researchers put it in the form of an article and send it to an academic journal for a blind peer review. The article is then sent out to a jury of one's peers with expertise in the field. They evaluate the study without knowing who did the study (hence the term *blind peer review*). The jury examines the theoretical or research-based context of the research question, the methodology, the statistical analysis (if it is a quantitative study), the interpretation of the data, and the conclusions of the researcher. Based on this, they (a) recommend the article be rejected, (b) suggest specific revisions be made and that it be resubmitted for consideration, (c) recommend it be published with revisions, or (d) recommend it be published. Highly prestigious academic journals have low acceptance rates, meaning that reviewers are extremely selective in deciding which studies get published.

Once published, the research is examined by the members within the field and the general public. Here, it is further analyzed, evaluated, critiqued, debated, and embraced or rejected. Journal articles are written supporting or denouncing the findings. Other research is carried out to replicate, reinforce, extend, or refute the findings. Tenure and promotion are earned, grants are awarded, fellowships are given, books are written, and guest appearances are made. This all leads to new questions and new research. Thus, the cycle of research life continues.

2. You Cannot Use Research to Say Anything You Want.

You can, however, misuse research to say anything you want. That is, you can find an outlier, a study that has not been peer reviewed, or a set of data that somebody has collected to support any particular point. Also, you can overinterpret or misinterpret research to make any point. This is a misuse of research. However, when you look at a body of research, you can clearly see general trends develop. This is why we generally do a review of the literature for our academic writing as opposed to a review of the study or a review of the article.

3. Research Is Used to Create Theories.

Theories help to organize relevant *empirical* facts in order to create a context for understanding phenomena (empirical means they can be observed or measured). A theory is a way to explain a set of facts. Put another way, if reality were a dot-to-dot picture, then a theory would be a way to connect a set of data dots. However, varying theories connect different data dots in different ways, resulting in a wide variety of pictures and practices. Thus, different theoretical perspectives can advocate different practices or practical notions even though each is based on a set of empirical data.

4. Research Does Not Prove Anything.

In an academic setting, research finds evidence to support a hypothesis or to state that a hypothesis is true with a degree of certainty. Research can also find no evidence to support a particular hypothesis. But research does not prove anything. It does not arrive at truth. Truth is a philosophical or meta-physical concept. Proofs only exist in the sterile world of mathematics, where outside variables do not exist. Instead, research supplies evidence to support theories. Theories are used to explain phenomena occurring in the natural world.

You can have a research-based practice, a validated practice, a practice that is supported by empirical evidence, or an evidenced-based practice, but you cannot have a practice that research has proven to be effective. Research supports and provides evidence; it does not prove. Even in the most con-trolled experimental research, there are far too many uncontrolled variables, many of which the researcher is unaware, to conclusively state that some-thing is proven true for all times and in all situations. Again, truth is a philosophical or metaphysical concept, not something that occurs in the physical world.

REFERENCES

Fraenkel, J., & Wallen, N. (2003). *How to design and evaluate research in education* (5th ed.). New York: McGraw-Hill.

Heath, S. B. (1983). *Ways with words: Language, life, and work in communities and classrooms.* New York: Cambridge University Press.

Jensen, E. (2009). *Teaching with poverty in mind.* Alexandria, VA: ASCD.

Johnson, A. (2012). *A short guide to action research* (4th ed.). Boston: Pearson Education.

National Assessment of Educational Progress (NAEP). (2014). *The nation's report card: 2013.* Retrieved from https://nces.ed.gov/nationsreportcard/reading/interpret_results.aspx

Sirin, S. R. (2005, Fall). Socioeconomic status and academic achievement: A meta-analytic review of research. *Review of Educational Research, 75,* 417–453.

Chapter Twenty-Three

Evaluating Research

Just because somebody says, "Research says . . ." does not mean that what follows is necessarily true or correct. In our personal and professional lives, we must learn to become critical consumers of research.

This chapter provides some basic tips for evaluating the research used in your academic writing. Also, being able to read and evaluate research will serve you well in your professional practice. Again, no single study should be the final word on anything. You will need to review many studies to get a sense of any topic in any field. Reviewing multiple studies from multiple perspectives provides context for your topic and also acts as a check on extreme or outlier positions.

HOW TO READ A RESEARCH ARTICLE

Most people do not read a research article straight through from front to back. It is recommended that you first skim the abstract to see if the study is related to your topic or question. If it is, then look at the research question and skim the results. This will provide you more information. Oftentimes, research articles are eliminated after these first two steps. That is, you find that an article does not fit exactly with your question or writing topic. If the research study is still of interest at this point, then read the literature review (before the methods section). This puts the research question in a theoretical context and will oftentimes point you toward other important articles or research. Also, the literature review will provide an indication as to what those in the field consider to be significant research and scholarly work. Finally, carefully review the methods, results, and conclusions.

Do not be discouraged if your initial reading and review of research articles seems slow and cumbersome. This is common. You get better at reading research articles by practice.

EVALUATING RESEARCH

There is no such thing as a perfect study. All research studies have strengths and limitations. The following five elements will enhance your ability to become a critical consumer of all types of research:

- *Researcher credibility:* Does the researcher's degree or current position indicate adequate knowledge in the particular field of research? Background knowledge is necessary to guide all phases of the inquiry. Expertise enables one to know what questions to ask, to see how new knowledge connects to existing knowledge, and to determine what's relevant and irrelevant.
- *Literature review:* New knowledge builds on existing knowledge. The literature review should provide a solid theoretical context and support for the research question or purpose of the study. It should also make a case for the importance of the study.
- *Research question or purpose:* The specific research question or the study purpose should flow directly from the literature review. Also, the research question or study purpose should be clearly stated and easy to understand. Everything that follows should be directly related to this question or purpose. At the end of the study, you should be able to answer yes or no as to whether the question has been answered or the purpose achieved.
- *Integrity:* It is impossible to be totally objective. Subjectivity can occur simply in deciding which questions to ask, which data to collect, and which measures to use to collect data. However, where there may be subjectivity or a conflict of interest, it should be stated up front by the researcher. Questions to ask here include: Does the study appear to be free of bias or hidden agendas? Are there groups who might benefit from a particular result? Is the researcher connected with a group that has a particular agenda? Does the researcher start with the answer and then look for data to support the answer?
- *Validity of the results or conclusions:* The conclusions, recommendations, or applications made at the end of a study should be confined only to that which can be supported by the data collected or described in this study. That is, they should come directly from and be supported by the data.

These elements should be considered when looking at any type of research. We turn now to specific elements to consider when evaluating quantitative and qualitative research.

QUANTITATIVE RESEARCH

Quantitative research focuses on collecting numerical data and isolating variables in order to explain, predict, or control phenomena of interest. This includes experimental research as well as correlational and causal-comparative research. The following elements pertain to research in the social sciences; however, the concepts can be applied to research in other areas.

Unequal Samples

You cannot compare things that are not comparable. If comparisons are being made, then the groups in a study must be similar in terms of demographics, ability, age, size, or other characteristics or variables. If not, then the interpretation of the results should be questioned. For example, if you are comparing public schools to private schools, then you must control for such things as abilities, socioeconomic status, parents' education levels, class sizes, and so on in order to make reasonable comparisons.

Sampling or Selection Bias

This occurs when the types of subjects included or excluded in a study could influence the results. For example, one group will always outperform another if low-performing subjects are underrepresented or high-performing individuals are overrepresented. Sampling bias systematically favors some outcome over another. Randomized selection to groups and matched samples are two common ways to avoid selection bias (see Chapter 22).

Unequal Treatment or Conditions

If comparisons are being made related to a treatment or condition, then there should be no significant differences other than the independent variable being examined. For example, in a study comparing Method A to Method B, if Method A was implemented sporadically, for shorter durations, and by less qualified people when compared with Method B, then the interpretation of the results should be questioned.

Size and Scope of the Subject Sample

Is the subject sample representative of the population to which it applies, or is it generalized? For example, if you did a study examining the effects of Treatment A on 25 elderly people in a small town, then it may be difficult to generalize to larger populations. The results could be germane to just elderly people, rural environments, the particular sample, or some other unaccounted variable. This does not mean that studies with limited subject samples are useless or invalid. Instead, they are limited in the types of generalizations that can be inferred from them.

The Mistaken Assumption of Homogeneity

You cannot assume that, because two groups or populations share a single variable, they are similar. For example, it would be difficult to make reasonable comparative conclusions between gun-owners in Boise, Idaho, and gun-owners in inner-city Los Angeles, California, because of the differences in environmental factors and a myriad of other uncontrolled variables. In the same way, it would be difficult to make comparative conclusions between reading instructional methods in a first-grade class in Grantsburg, Wisconsin, and a first-grade class in Apply Valley, Minnesota. There are simply too many unaccounted variables. Descriptive studies that generalize to larger groups based on single-variable comparisons between groups should be questioned.

Clearly Described Population

You should be critical of any research in which the researcher does not clearly describe the populations or subjects involved.

Statistical Significance

Statistical significance means the difference is more than could happen by chance. If the difference between groups is slight, then the difference could simply be a matter of chance. This means, for small groups, you need to see large differences. For large groups, you can see smaller differences. Always look to see if the differences between groups or measures are statistically significant.

Validity of the Measure

Do the measures used for the dependent variable actually account for that which it claims to measure? Is it a valid measure of that trait or attribute? For example, you can get very accurate and reliable data pertaining to people's abilities to run 100 meters, but would this be a valid measure of their abilities to play tennis or football? In education, we often see the question of validity arise when scores on achievement tests are used to demonstrate learning, teacher effectiveness, reading ability, ability to learn, or some other variable beyond the very narrow scope of the standardized measure.

QUALITATIVE RESEARCH

Qualitative research focuses on understanding naturally occurring phenomena in real-life settings. It uses systematic observations to study and come to understand people, places, events, situations, and experiences with all their many variables in all their complexity (Johnson, 2012). The following are seven elements to consider when evaluating qualitative research (Leedy & Ormrod, 2010):

Detachment.

You should get the sense that the researcher is not attached to a particular view and is willing to let the data speak. That is, the researcher does not start with the answer. Instead, the researcher allows the data collected to inform or change his or her views.

Rigor.

The plan for collecting and analyzing data should be systematic and described in a way that invites duplication. Also, the number of observations, their duration, and the quantity of data collected should be sufficient to understand what is being studied. The duration of the study should also be such that enough data can be collected to adequately answer the research question or address the study purpose.

Data depth and breadth.

The type of data collected should be sufficient to adequately answer the research question or contribute to the purpose of the study. Also, multiple types of data should be collected over time.

Accuracy and completeness.

The description should provide an accurate and complete picture of the person, place, event, situation, or experience being studied. All relevant aspects of the environments should be described in a way that enables a thorough understanding of the phenomena being studied.

Coherence.

You should be able to easily read and understand the research report. It should make sense. The literature review, research question, methodology, findings, and discussion or conclusion should all be aligned. Each of these should build on the previous element.

Logic and persuasiveness.

The researcher should use sound logic to analyze and interpret the data. Also, the findings, conclusions, or recommendations should be a logical extension or application of the data.

Usefulness.

The findings should be able to be used to enhance your understanding of similar people, places, events, situations, or experiences.

THE LAST WORD

This chapter provides just a brief overview of how to evaluate research in the social sciences. Many of the concepts can also be applied to research in other areas. Again, there is no such thing as a perfect study or experiment.

REFERENCES

Johnson, A. (2012). *A short guide to action research* (4th ed.). Boston: Pearson.
Leedy, P. D., & Ormrod, J. E. (2010). *Practical research: Planning and design* (9th ed.). Boston: Pearson.

Chapter Twenty-Four

Describing Research

Research provides the data-dots on which theories are built.

Research descriptions can be used in all parts of your academic writing, but most often they are used in a formal literature review. Descriptions of research are also used in preparing an annotated bibliography and in writing research proposals (described in the next chapter). Finally, looking for and understanding these elements will be helpful in your own analysis and understanding of research.

THE ELEMENTS

When describing research studies, describe each of these elements in the following order:

Question or purpose of the study: Use one sentence to describe the research question or study purpose.

Subjects or participants: Use as few sentences as possible (usually one to three) to describe the subjects or participants. Include the number of subjects or participants, any relevant demographic information, and any other characteristics that are germane to the study, such as age, socioeconomic status, educational level, gender, and so on.

Treatment, criteria, or conditions: For quantitative studies, describe the independent variable. This would be the approach, treatment, or element that the researcher was trying to manipulate or isolate. For descriptive research, describe the criteria used to select the various data used for analysis. For qualitative research, describe the general setting, environment, or conditions in which the data were observed or collected.

Measures or instruments: Describe which data were collected (dependent variable), how they were collected, and what was used to collect them.

Results or findings: Describe the relevant results in a quantitative study or findings in a qualitative study. Also, describe in very general terms what the results or findings might mean.

Limitations: As stated in the last chapter, there's no such thing as the perfect study. If there are significant limitations to the study, then these should be described.

EXAMPLES

The following are some examples how to describe research. The first example uses simplistic, nonsense studies so that the elements stand out:

Fruit
This section describes two studies related to fruit.

Manning Study
Manning (2015) examined the effects of pomegranates on working memory. For this study, 57 subjects were chosen from a pool of 150 college students and randomly assigned to either a treatment or control group. The treatment group ate 3 pomegranates each day for 27 weeks. The control group ate no pomegranates. Both groups took the Dabrowski Memory Test as a posttreatment measure. It was found that the experimental group scored significantly higher than the nonpomegranate control group in this measure. It may be inferred that pomegranates may have a positive effect on memory.

Bridgewater and Manning Study
Bridgewater and Manning (2014) wanted to see if nectarines had any effect on reasoning ability. The subjects for this study were 261 adults selected from a sample population and randomly put into treatment and control groups. The Jones Reasoning Test was given as a pretreatment measure. There were no statistically significant differences between the two groups on this measure. Over a 6-month period, the treatment group was given 3.5 cups of chopped nectarines to eat each day. The control group ate no nectarines during this time. Posttreatment measures showed no differences between the two groups.

Summary of Fruit Studies
The results of the studies reviewed are summarized here:
• Bananas have been shown to positively affect memory (Manning, 2015).
• Nectarines appear to have no significant effect on reasoning ability (Bridgewater & Manning, 2014).

The following is an example of a fairly complicated study. In your description, it is not necessary to include every aspect of the study. A study may produce a variety of results. Report only the results that are of importance to your writing topic.

Winston and Mariota Study

Winston and Mariota (2015) compared the effectiveness of an instructional program related to small-group study strategies to an instructional program related to individual study skills on student learning as well as the acquisition and transfer of study skills.

The subjects for this study consisted of 227 first-year college students enrolled in two general education courses in the liberal arts. Three separate sections of each course were taught by the same instructor to two different treatment groups and one control group. Instruction and practice for the two treatment groups consisted of weekly 45-minute sessions spread over 15 weeks as part of class. Specially trained instructors were used just for the study skills instruction in each course. Course content was used for instruction and practice.

Treatment Group A was given instruction and activities that taught strategies for studying in pairs and small groups. Treatment Group B was given instruction and activities that taught individual study skills. No extra instruction or activities were provided to the control group.

Dependent variables consisted of average scores on course exams. To assess learning over time, students were tracked over the next 3 semesters. Scores on similar course exams in general education courses were recorded and compared. To assess the acquisition and transfer of study skills, a Likert-type rating scale where students reacted to various dimensions of their own performance studying for exams were given 6 times over the succeeding 3 semesters. As part of this, students were also asked to describe the processes used to study.

Mean score averages for each course showed statistically significant differences favoring the two treatment groups over the control. There were no statistically significant differences between treatment groups. Comparisons of scores over the next 3 semesters, however, showed statistically significant differences favoring Treatment Group A over the other groups on mean average scores for course exams. Also, Likert scores and self-reports showed statistically significant differences favoring Treatment Group A in the retention and use of study skills as well students' perceived success in studying.

These results seem to suggest that study skill strategy instruction can be useful in enhancing learning for college students and that instruction related to small-group study skills may be the most effective in retaining and using study skills over time. The researchers speculated that the interpersonal elements may have contributed to students' initial learning and continued use of these various study skills.

THE LAST WORD

There are three things you might take away from the previous example: First, to be able to effectively describe a study, you have to have a good understanding of all its components. A strategy to use when reading a study like this is to create a simple template with each of the elements (see Figure 24.1). As you read the study, record the important information using enumeration or an outline under each element.

Figure 24.1. Template for Reading and Understanding Research

Author, date, title, journal:

Question or purpose of the study:

Subjects or participants:

Treatment, criteria, or conditions:

Measures or instruments:

Results or findings:

Limitations:

Second, keep in mind that you are writing to an audience who has no familiarity with the study. Assume the reader knows nothing. You have to be very clear and concise in your description. You do not have to replicate all aspects of the study, but you should accurately represent the salient features.

The last thing: Notice the language that was used in describing the earlier results. Results for research are usually reported using such soft terms as *suggests, seems to indicate, provides support for, may be,* and *points to.* Rarely will you see terms like *proves* or *shows that, verifies, validates, confirms,* or *demonstrates.* This is because research does not prove anything to be true. Experimental research supports or does not support a null hypothesis, or it answers a specific research question. Qualitative research leads to a greater understanding of people, places, events, situations, and experiences. Each bit of research identifies certain elements that can be used to support, expand, or add to the larger theoretical dot-to-dot picture. Theories are designed to evolve and eventually become obsolete as new information is discovered and new theories emerge.

Chapter Twenty-Five

The Annotated Bibliography and Research Proposal

An annotated bibliography emerges naturally from a well-defined topic or question.

An annotated bibliography is a list of reviewed sources followed by a short description or annotation of each. This review could include research studies as well as any of the other types of sources described in Chapter 2.

PURPOSE

There are four general purposes for an annotated bibliography. First, an annotated bibliography can be helpful in preparing for a large research paper or project. It invites you to read more critically and to organize your sources so that you can find the structure necessary for your literature review. The annotated bibliography also provides a sense of perspective or overview of your research topic.

Second, outside a writing context, annotated bibliographies can be useful if you need to be informed about a program, policy, practice, or procedure. It puts important information together in an organized fashion so that you can easily see and refer to the key points, authors, dates, and journals.

Third, some form of an annotated bibliography is usually included in research or grant proposals. (I have included a sample proposal here.) Proposals for a master's thesis or doctoral dissertation demonstrate to your advisor or committee that you have done a general survey of the literature, that there is sufficient research and theoretical support for your question or topic, and that you have the background knowledge necessary to proceed. Also, the studies reviewed can inform and shape your research questions as well as methodology.

And finally, an annotated bibliography is sometimes used to provide an overview of research in a particular area or on a particular topic.

HOW TO CREATE AN ANNOTATED BIBLIOGRAPHY

Step 1: Read and Take Notes.

Start with one of your sources, critically read it, and take notes (see Chapter 2).

Step 2: Review and Identify the Salient Points.

If you are annotating a research study, then this is fairly straightforward (see Chapter 24). Annotating a theoretical article is not as clear. Here, you will need to identify and synthesize what you believe to be the essential and relevant ideas. This is a bit different from note-taking, where you simply record all ideas of interest or relevance. There is not uniformity in this process or in what the end product looks like. Each person's understanding and interpretation of a theoretical article will be a bit different based on his or her own experience, motive for reading, and writing topic or question.

To demonstrate this process, Frank read and took notes on the following Palmer (2003) article. However, his notes contained too many ideas and did not enable him to accurately capture and describe the essence of the article. He went back to the original article, reread it, and captured what he thought were nine important ideas:

> Palmer, P. J. (2003). Teaching with heart and soul: Reflections on spirituality in teacher education. *Journal of Teacher Education, 54,* 376–385.

1. Defines spiritual in a sacred sense as an eternal yearning to be connected with something larger than your own ego.
2. Spiritual crisis = we find ourselves in the grip of something larger than the ego's needs.
3. Language of the heart and soul has many names. We can use a term from depth psychology, individuation, to understand this in a sacred sense. Education of the heart and soul.
4. Education that addresses inner issues leads to empowerment and individuation. We are less apt to be shaped, influenced by secular, economic, and political needs of groups and more likely to be shaped by Self or higher self or motives. Our own higher aspirations.
5. Liberal arts education seeks to liberate the mind. We can and must include this in teacher education programs.

6. Education of individuation in teacher education provides preservice teachers with the resources to face their own soul-challenging experience, as well as the resources to help their students develop the full potential and face similar challenges.

7. Dispersing data (information, skills, and concepts) without meaning or connections to self and bigger ideas, creates a soulless experience that serves to alienate and dulls.

8. Relationships between the teacher and students must be deeply human for learning to occur.

9. Palmer recommends that teachers groups are created called Courage to Teach (CTT) for educators in which inner-life issues are addressed.

Step 3: Begin Writing.

Your goal here is to create a cohesive yet concise overview of the source that accurately depicts the relevant ideas. This is usually one to three paragraphs in length. Keep in mind that you are writing to an audience who has not read the article. Thus, you may need to include some additional explanation to elucidate and connect ideas. You may also need to move some ideas around. That is, they may be presented in your annotation in a different order than they appeared in the source. Finally, in writing this overview, you may find, as Frank did here, that some ideas that you included in Step 2 do not add to the clarity of your annotation and, thus, should not be included:

Palmer, P. J. (2003). Teaching with heart and soul: Reflections on spirituality in teacher education. *Journal of Teacher Education, 54,* 376–385.

Palmer defines *spirituality* in a sacred sense as an eternal yearning to be connected with something larger than your own ego. He posits that spirituality, what he calls the language of the heart and soul, should be addressed in a secular sense in our K–12 schools and teacher education programs. Using a term from depth psychology, this would be individuation. Individuation is to understand and embrace your inner self (Self) in order to achieve your full potential. Including inner issues in both teacher education and K–12 education is a means toward this end.

Education of individuation addresses inner issues and can lead to individuation and empowerment. Here we are less likely to be shaped and influenced by the social, economic, emotional, or political needs of others and more likely to be influenced by our own ideals or Self. Toward this end, liberal arts education, one that seeks to liberate the mind by addressing inner issues, can and must be included in teacher education programs.

The education of individuation in teacher education programs provides preservice teachers with the resources necessary to face their own soul-challenging experiences. It also provides them with the resources to help their future students individuate and face similar challenges. We must move beyond simply dispersing data or teaching knowledge and skills without connection to greater meaning. This creates a soulless experience that serves only to alienate and dull students and teachers and impedes their path to individuation.

As part of Step 3, reread and revise your annotations several times. These descriptions must be extremely concise and tightly written.

Step 4: Move on to the Next Source and Repeat the Process.

Step 5: Organize Into Groups.

The last step is to organize your individual annotations into sections or groups related to topics. For example, if Frank's topic were the professional development of teachers, the previous annotation would most likely go into a section related to inner development or inner dimensions. Some sources call for an annotated bibliography to be organized alphabetically. This may be preferable if you are annotating only a few sources.

ANNOTATED BIBLIOGRAPHY AS PART OF A RESEARCH PROPOSAL

An annotated bibliography is often used as part of research proposal. The following proposal is for a teacher action research project (Johnson, 2012). You can see how the annotated bibliography emerges naturally from the topic. Also, the research questions and the methodology were informed and shaped by the studies reviewed in the annotated bibliography:

Proposal for Action Research Project
Department Special Education
Arthur B. Student
July 15, 2016

This is a proposal for my action research project. I plan to conduct this research project from May 5 to May 23, 2016.

Topic

The topic for this action research project is low-ability math students and their use of math dialogue journals (MDJ).

Annotated Bibliography

This section describes two studies related to dialogue journals:

Smith study. Smith (2015) examined the effects of dialogue journals on students' understanding of psychology. For this study, 40 subjects were chosen from a pool of 150 college psychology students and randomly assigned to either a treatment or control group. The treatment group used dialogue journals with daily journal prompts and weekly responses from instructors. The control group was given the same instruction experience without the use of journals. At the end of the semester, both groups took the Eggens Comprehensive Psychology Test as a posttreatment measure. It was found that the experimental group scored significantly higher than the control group in this measure. It may be inferred that dialogue journals have some positive effect on students' understanding of complex concepts related to psychology.

Jacobson and Smith study. Jacobson and Smith (2014) wanted to see if dialogue journals had any effect on students' reasoning ability. The subjects for this study were 82 adults selected from a college introductory psychology course. They were randomly assigned to treatment and control groups. The Jenson Reasoning Test was given as a pretreatment measure and showed no statistically significant differences between the two groups. Over a 2-month period, the treatment group was given real-life reasoning problems for them to solve each week. Students were asked to solve the problem and explain their reasoning along with any questions or confusion they had. Research assistants would collect the journals and respond to students' entries. During this time, the control group was given the same problem and simply asked to answer it. Their answers were simply evaluated as being right or wrong. At the end of 2 months, the Jenson Reasoning Test was again given. Posttreatment measures showed significant difference favoring the experimental group on this measure. It appears that dialogue journals used with instructor's response seems to have a positive effect on students' ability to solve these logical thinking problems.

Summary of dialogue journals studies. The studies reviewed seem to indicate the following:

1. Dialogue journals seemed to positively affect students' understanding of complex psychology concepts (Smith, 2015).

2. Dialogue journals used to solve reasoning problems seem to have a significant effect on students' ability to think logically (Jacobson & Smith, 2014).

Application. These two studies both examine the effects of dialogue journals. They tell me that dialogue journals can be used to guide or enhance students' understanding and thinking abilities. These are both important elements of learning how to understand and apply mathematics. I think the important part of this will be the response that I give students. This will be used to guide students' thought processes as well as clear up confusion.

Questions

The research questions I am interested in are:

1. How do MDJs work with my low-ability math students?

2. Are MDJs effective in helping my students' ability to understand math processes?

3. Do students find MDJs helpful or enjoyable?

Methodology

This section describes the methodology used in this action research project:

Participants. There will be 12 fifth-grade students participating in this study. They are 11 and 12 years old. Eight are male, and 4 are female. They are all part of my afternoon, low-ability homogeneous math class.

Materials. Each student will be using a regular 8" × 10.5" notebook as an MDJ. Also used in this study will be a student survey. This survey will contain five Likert-like questions that ask students to rate the effectiveness of various aspects of the MDJ as well as three open-ended questions (see Appendix A)

Data. Data collected will be students' MDJs, teacher field notes, and student surveys. The MDJs will be collected after 3 weeks. Here, students' responses and my comments will be analyzed. Daily lesson plans will be used to record my field notes. At the end of each lesson, I will use the back of the lesson plan to record my general observations and noticeable events, as well as procedures that seem to be effective or less effective. Finally, a survey will be given to students to assess their perception of the MDJs.

Procedures. We are currently using MDJs with my fifth-grade math class. We use them three ways. First, they are used for scaffolded instruction. As I introduce a new procedure, students go through the steps with me, using their math journals to record each step. Second, in small groups, students explain the steps to each other and then record the instruction in their words in their journals. Students are also encouraged to use pictures or diagrams to help them remember or understand math procedures. And third, at the end of class, I ask students to record two clear ideas and two fuzzy ideas. This allows me to engage in a direct written dialogue with students. I also have students record their own homework scores.

After math class, students put their journals in a milk crate on the shelf. This keeps the journals from being lost or used for other purposes. It also enables me to have daily access to them. I generally try to respond to three MDJs every day. This enables me to give a very personal response to each student every 4 days.

For this study, I will select a 3-week period to examine and analyze. Everything in my math class will be run as I normally would during this period with the exception that I will use the back of the daily lesson plans for in-depth reflection and students will be given a survey at the end of the 3 weeks.

Organization and analysis of data. In examining students' MDJs, I will be looking to see if I notice patterns or reoccurring themes. I will be looking to see how they use their MDJs and what sorts of things they put in them. I will also be looking for patterns and the quality of student responses in the comments I have written in their journals. If possible, inductive analysis will be used to find and describe grouping patterns and numbers within each group.

The field notes will also be examined for emerging patterns. I will also look to see if there are any relationships between my observations and student responses in their MDJs.

The survey will contain quantifiable data as well as open-ended comments. Average scores will be determined for each question that uses the Likert response. I will look for reoccurring patterns to emerge on the open-ended responses. If possible, inductive analysis will be used to find and describe grouping patterns and numbers within each group.

Appendix A
Student Survey

5 = strongly agree, 4 = agree, 3 = neutral or don't know, 2 = disagree, 1 = strongly disagree

1. Math dialogue journals help me understand math.
     5 . . . . 4 . . . . 3 . . . . 2 1

2. Math dialogue journals are a waste of time.
     5 . . . . 4 . . . . 3 . . . . 2 1

3. Math dialogue journals make math class more enjoyable.
     5 . . . . 4 . . . . 3 . . . . 2 1

4. Math dialogue journals make math more confusing.
     5 . . . . 4 . . . . 3 . . . . 2 1

5. I like seeing the teacher's comments in my math dialogue journal.
   5 . . . . 4 . . . . 3 . . . . 2 1

6. I do not like using math dialogue journals.
   5 . . . . 4 . . . . 3 . . . . 2 1

7. What do you like about using math dialogue journals?

8. What don't you like about using math dialogue journals?

9. If you could change something about using math dialogue journals, what would it be?

REFERENCES

Johnson, A. (2012). *A short guide to action research* (4th ed.). Boston: Pearson.
Palmer, P. J. (2003). Teaching with heart and soul: Reflections on spirituality in teacher education. *Journal of Teacher Education, 54,* 376–385.

Chapter Twenty-Six

The Literature Review

It's all about the process.

THE PROCESS

This chapter focuses on the process of creating a literature review and not simply a description of what the product should look like. What appears on the page is only part of the literature review process. And without understanding the process, you will struggle mightily with the product. This process is briefly described in Chapter 2. This chapter revisits, expands on, and demonstrates some aspects of it.

An Operational Definition

A literature review is a synthesis of your sources related to your writing or research topic. It critically examines and reviews what the literature says about your topic and describes it in an organized fashion. In a research study, the literature review typically appears before the research question and methods section. In a theoretical article, it typically appears before the application, recommendations, conclusions, or summary.

Purpose

Depending on the type of academic writing, a literature review serves one or more of the following purposes:

1. It provides a theoretical and research-based context for what follows.
2. It defines and clarifies your writing topic.
3. It informs the reader of the current state of your topic.

4. It describes common themes, concepts, or ideas found in the literature.
5. It integrates knowledge found within and across disciplines.
6. It enhances the understanding of new knowledge.
7. It brings new insight to existing knowledge.
8. It leads to the novel applications of existing knowledge.
9. It suggests possible uses for existing knowledge to solve real-world problems.
10. It identifies contradictions, gaps, and inconsistencies in the literature.

Quantity of Sources

How many sources should you review for your literature review? A formal literature review for a doctoral dissertation or master's thesis should be fairly substantial. Check with your advisor or committee for guidance here. A literature review used for most academic papers, journal articles, annotated bibliographies, research projects, and other forms of academic writing typically uses fewer sources than a dissertation or thesis.

Two guiding principles:

1. Your goal is to see what all the literature says about your topic and to become a knowledgeable expert. This expertise should be reflected in your writing. The number of sources used varies on the level and type of writing. However, more sources are always better than fewer.
2. The literature should be used to guide and inform you. Do not start with the answer. That is, do not simply search for sources to support a predetermined conclusion. This is subjectivity by omission and inclusion, and it is not a good thing in academic writing. Instead, let the data speak.

Form

The literature review needs some type of an organizing structure (see Chapters 3 and 14). Two basic organizing structures are described here.

Inverted Triangle. An inverted triangle is a structure that moves from general to specific knowledge. Here the literature review ends with a tight focus on your topic or research question. Having an initial flexible structure like this in place *before* you begin looking for sources can be used to guide your search.

For example, Sam was writing an article on the effect of emotions on learning to read. Going from general to specific, he used the following organizing structure to guide his initial search:

1. Emotions.
2. Learning.

3. Emotions and learning.
4. Emotions and learning to read.

In his article, he started by describing emotions from a cognitive and neurological perspective. Then, he described learning from a cognitive and neurological perspective. Next, he described the specific impact of emotions on learning, focusing on cognitive functions. Finally, he described the effect of emotions on learning to read. He was then able to use the remainder of the article to describe specific recommendations for practice based on the literature review.

Emerging Structure (Skeleton). As described in Chapter 3, you can also allow for the structure to emerge from your sources. During the predrafting phase, after you have read your sources and taken notes, look for patterns, themes, or common ideas to emerge from your data. Begin putting these data into groups. These initial groupings should be very flexible. As you get more information, these often change. Then look for a superordinate and subordinate structure for your groups, sometimes called sections and subsections. This initial organizing structure can then be used to guide you in writing your first draft as well as searching for additional sources.

In the following example, Alice was writing a paper describing the reading process from a neurological perspective. As she was reviewing her sources and taking notes, she began to see some initial groups emerge. After she moved data into these initial groupings, she created three sections to organize her groups: (a) Understanding Reading, (b) Reading: A Neurological Process, and (c) The Neurocognitive Processes. These initial sections and subsections helped guide her continued search. That is, they showed Alice where she had gaps and inconsistencies that needed additional sources to clarify:

CREATING MEANING WITH PRINT: THE NEUROCOGNITIVE MODEL
I. Understanding Reading
  1. The Phonological Processing Model of Reading
  2. The Neurocognitive Model of Reading
  3. Creating Meaning with Print
II. Reading: A Neurological Perspective
  1. The Three Cuing Systems
  3. The Relative Unimportance of Letters
III. The Neurocognitive Processes
  1. A Transactive Process
  2. Speed and Efficiency
  3. The Meaninglessness of Individual Words

As Alice continued to gather sources, take notes, write a first draft, and revise, some of her initial groups merged, some changed, and others were eliminated. Her structure was a flexible, dynamic entity that continued to evolve with new data. However, this structure eventually solidified and was used for her paper.

SAMPLE LITERATURE REVIEW

The following is a sample of Alice's paper that was written using the previous structure:

The Neurocognitive Processes

As visual data is taken in from the eyes, it moves to the relay station in the brain called the thalamus. All three cuing systems are then used to make sense of this data before it moves to the cortex. The cortex is the part of the brain responsible for higher-level thinking and memory. A system here is not a particular location or part of the brain but a series of interconnected parts or regions (Fischer, Immordino-Yang, & Waber, 2007; Xu, Kemeny, Park, Frattali, & Bran, 2005).

A Transactive Process

However, information does not flow just one way from the page to the thalamus and up to the cortex. Brain imaging research shows that, as we process data taken in by the various senses, information also flows from the cortex down to the thalamus (Engel, Fries, & Singer, 2001; Hawkins, 2004; Hruby, 2009; Koch, 2004). In fact, there is almost 10 times more information flowing down from the cortex to the thalamus than up from the thalamus to the cortex (Alitto & Usrey, 2003; Destexhe, 2000; Gilbert & Sigman, 2007; Koch, 2004; Sherman & Guillery, 2004; Strauss, 2011). This means that higher structures of the brain (those involved in thought and reasoning), control or influence the lower structures during the act of processing visual information (Ducket, 2008; Gilbert & Sigman, 2007; Hawkins, 2004).

QUESTIONS

Put your writing topic in the form of one or more general questions before you begin. This will enhance your efficiency and effectiveness when selecting and evaluating sources, and it can provide an initial structure for your writing. For example, Steven was very much interested in the topic of mental health issues for adolescents. Having first identified a topic, he then created the following four questions: (a) Are there significant problems related to adolescents and mental health? (b) If so, what are they, and how prevalent are they? (c) What are the most common issues or problems? (d) What are some strategies that are effective in addressing mental health problems with adolescents?

Putting his topic in the form of these questions created a specific purpose for reading that was used to guide his source selection, reading, and note-taking. He was able to quickly scan and look for sources specifically related to his questions. He only kept those that addressed his questions. Also, during reading, he found himself reading to find something specific. This is much different than simply reading to see what something says. And, when he was evaluating ideas for note-taking, he only recorded data that specifically addressed his questions. You will find that creating specific questions related to your writing topic will enhance the efficiency and effectiveness of all parts of the first stage of writing. This does not mean that you're locked into these questions, but it does provide an initial structuring focus.

THE LAST WORD

The following is a quick review of the steps used in the literature review process: (a) Put your topic in the form of a question, (b) gather sources, (c) read and take careful notes, (d) look for groups to emerge, (d) organize your data into groups, (e) organize your groups into sections and subsections, (f) create the first extremely rough draft, and (g) revise and repeat steps as necessary.

REFERENCES

Alitto, H. J., & Usrey, W. M. (2003). Corticothalamic feedback and sensory processing. *Current Opinion in Neurobiology, 13,* 440–445.

Destexhe, A. (2000). Modeling corticothalamic feedback and the gating of the thalamus by the cerebral corrects. *Journal of Physiology, 94,* 394–410.

Ducket, P. (2008). Seeing the story for the words: The eye movements of beginning readers. In A. Flurky, E. Paulson, & K. Goodman (Eds.), *Scientific realism in studies of reading* (pp. 113–128). New York: LEA.

Engel, A. K., Fries, P., & Singer, W. (2001). Dynamic predictions: Oscillations and synchrony in top-down processing. *Nature Reviews Neuroscience, 2,* 704–716.

Fischer, K. W., Immordino-Yang, M. H., & Waber, D. (2007). Toward a grounded synthesis of mind, brain, and education for reading disorders: An introduction to the field and this book. In K. Fischer, J. H. Bernstein, & M. H. Immordino-Yang (Eds.), *Mind, brain, and education in reading disorders* (pp. 3–15). New York: Cambridge University Press.

Gilbert, C. S., & Sigman, M. (2007). Brain states: Top-down influence in sensory processing. *Neuron, 54,* 667–696.

Hawkins, J. (2004). *On intelligence.* New York: Henry Holt.

Hruby, G. G. (2009). Grounding reading comprehension in the neuroscience literatures. In S. E. Israel & G. P. Duffy (Eds.), *Handbook of research on reading comprehension* (pp. 189–223). New York: Routledge.

Johnson, A. (2016). *10 essential instruction elements for students with reading difficulties: a brain friendly approach.* Thousand Oaks, CA: Corwin.

Koch, C. (2004). *The quest for consciousness: A neurobiological approach.* Englewood, CO: Roberts.

Sherman, S. M., & Guillery, R. W. (2004). The visual relays in the thalamus. In L. M. Chalupa & J. S. Werner (Eds.), *The visual neurosciences* (pp. 565–591). Cambridge, MA: MIT Press.

Strauss, S. L. (2011). Neuroscience and dyslexia. In A. McGill-Franzen & R. L. Allington (Eds.), *Handbook of reading disability research* (pp. 79–90). New York: Routledge.

Xu, J., Kemeny, S., Park, G., Frattali, C., & Bran, A. (2005). Language in context: Emergent features of word, sentence, and narrative comprehension. *Neuroimage, 25,* 1002–1015.

V

Theses and Dissertations

Chapter Twenty-Seven

Secondary Research

The only good thesis or dissertation is a completed thesis or dissertation.

This chapter describes the elements of a master's-level thesis and doctoral dissertation involving secondary research. The next chapter describes these elements when doing primary research.

SOME PROCESS TIPS

These tips will help to facilitate the process of writing a thesis or dissertation for both secondary and original research. Some of these are a review of things covered in earlier chapters:

1. Before beginning your project, make sure you are familiar with specific guidelines and instructions for your institution. Universities all have varying requirements here.
2. See your advisor before beginning. Make sure you have a clear understanding of your advisor's expectations. Ask a lot of questions about the process and the product. Remember, your advisor has done this before.
3. Listen to your advisor. This is not *your* thesis or dissertation exactly; instead, this is a thesis or dissertation that you are doing under the guidance of your advisor. Your advisor will have the final say, as he or she will ultimately have to sign off on this. Listening to your advisor will enhance the efficiency and effectiveness of all your efforts.
4. Give yourself plenty of time to complete this project. This tip has been stated elsewhere in this book, and with a project this large, it is particularly important. Research projects at this level take a great deal of

time to think, plan, read, and revise. For this, you should be thinking in terms of months, not weeks.

5. First identify a problem or decide on a topic for your research. Focus only on this step initially. Do not worry about anything else at this point.

6. Once you have identified a problem or topic, put it in the form of a preliminary question or questions. Revise your question to make it as concise and precise as possible. However, keep in mind that it is common for your initial question to evolve or change as you begin reading and getting background information for your project.

7. Understand the basic process. Whether you are doing primary or secondary research, you are essentially asking a question and looking for data to answer your question. This is why it is important to craft a precisely worded question to begin the process.

8. Start in a state of unknowing. Do not start with the answer and look for data to support your predetermined question. This is not research. Do not set out to prove something. This is not how academic inquiry works. Even if you think you know the answer to your question, you must let the data speak to you. This is the mind-set needed to successfully engage in the thesis or dissertation process and to complete this project.

9. Stay objective. You are not promoting any particular strategy, method, approach, policy, procedure, program, or agenda. You are asking and answering a question. You can make recommendations based on your data at specific places in your thesis or dissertation; however, we should only see these at the appropriate places (see later).

10. Do not expect your advisor to edit. Your advisor will provide feedback and some editorial comments, but an advisor is much different from an editor. The onus is ultimately on you to write in a logical, coherent, objective style.

11. Plan on revising each chapter a minimum of four times (although it will usually be more than this).

12. Put this project in perspective. This tip is most relevant for those working on a dissertation. There are some who have not completed their dissertations because they thought they had to get it just right. Instead, get it done. The only good dissertation is a completed dissertation. There is no distinction in being ABD (all but dissertation). The completed dissertation (or thesis) is your ticket for moving on to the next stage in your professional life. This will not be the final word on your topic, and this will not be your defining personal or professional statement. You will be doing other more significant work later.

13. Focus on and embrace the process. The thesis and dissertation is about understanding the process of asking and answering academic

questions. The actual product you create (thesis or dissertation) is important. It enables you to add to the literature on a particular topic. However, the process is what you will take with you and what you will utilize all your professional life.

Primary and secondary research both involve the process of asking and answering questions. Whereas primary research involves generating original data to answer a question, secondary research uses data gleaned by others in the form of journal articles and other academic sources to answer a question. Theses or dissertations using secondary research have four chapters. The elements of each are here.

CHAPTER I: INTRODUCTION

This chapter is relatively short (three to eight pages in length). Start by introducing the topic (no heading for this section). Identify the problem, provide background information, and connect to the larger world.

Problem Statement

Use a centered heading. State the problem and the purpose of the paper:

- Example: The purpose of this paper is to review current literature related to self-selected approaches to spelling instruction and to describe effective implementation practices.

Then, put the purpose in the form of one or more questions:

- Example: The specific research questions are:
1. Is a self-selected approach to spelling instruction effective in developing students' ability to spell correctly under real-life writing conditions?
2. If so, how should a self-selected approach to spelling instruction be implemented in an elementary school setting?

Importance of the Study

Use a centered heading. Tell why the project is important and to whom:

- Example: The information here will be of value to general education and special education teachers at the elementary level for. . . . It will also provide elementary teachers with a framework to use in designing a research-based approach to. . . .

Methodology

Use a centered heading. Tell how the data were selected and which criteria were used to select the data:

- Example: Data were collected using recognized, academic journals. Each journal was peer reviewed and printed no earlier than 2005. Texts written by recognized experts in the field were also used.

Limitations of the Study

Use a centered heading. Describe the limitations or applicability of the results. For example, can it be applied only to a certain segment of the population? Were you able to look at all facets of the problem?

Definition of Terms

Use a centered heading. Briefly define the important terms the reader will encounter in the review of the literature.

Headings

Use third-level headings for each term (bold-faced, indented five spaces, a capital letter on the first letter of the first word, a period at the end, and begin the description on the same line).

Description Length

Descriptions are in glossary form and are one or two sentences in length. Use complete sentences here.

Figure 27.1   Chapter I

CHAPTER I
INTRODUCTION

Problem Statement

Importance of the Study

Methodology

Limitations of the Study

Definition of Terms

CHAPTER II: REVIEW OF THE LITERATURE

This chapter contains a review of the literature related to your topic as described earlier in this book. This is the heart of the secondary research project. Include only information that is necessary to answer your research question. Create structure as described earlier using headings and subheadings. This chapter ends with a brief summary of the major points covered. This summary can be in list form or described in one to three paragraphs.

CHAPTER III: APPLICATION

Select and synthesize relevant information from Chapter II to create or design an application. Your application should answer some or all of the following questions: What are your recommendations? How should this knowledge be used? What is your plan? What should it look like? How should it work? How might others use it? Do not include new information here; rather, use only ideas that are based on information presented in Chapter II. Assume the role of the expert. Use headings and subheadings to create structure. Cite when necessary.

CHAPTER IV: SUMMARY AND CONCLUSIONS

This chapter should also be relatively short (three to eight pages in length). You should not introduce any new information or ideas here. Start with a short review of the purpose of the paper, and restate the research question or questions. Do not using headings for the first section of this chapter.

Summary

Use a centered heading. Summarize the important points from Chapters II and III. The presentation of ideas here should be in the same order as they appear in Chapters II and III. These may be in list form or described in one or two short paragraphs.

Conclusions

Use a centered heading. Describe the specific ideas or conclusions you have as a result of the information found in Chapters II and III. Explain the implications of the findings to other situations, populations, and education settings.

Recommendations

Use a centered heading. Describe your recommendations or how the information should be used. This should be a brief restatement or overview of your application from Chapter III. Note that "Conclusions" and "Recommendations" sometimes merge into one section.

Figure 27.2   Chapter IV

CHAPTER IV
SUMMARY AND CONCLUSIONS

Summary

Conclusions

Methodology

Recommendations

REFERENCES

Reference citations are listed in alphabetical order by authors' last names. Do not include extra spaces between citations.

APPENDIXES

Appendixes are not required. However, they are used to provide detailed information that would be distracting to read in the main body of the article. Do not include any commercially available material here.

THE LAST WORD

It's always helpful to look at a finished product. You can find plenty of examples of completed theses and dissertations on the Internet with minimal effort. Completed theses and dissertations are also often housed in university libraries.

Chapter Twenty-Eight

Primary Research

The best tip for completing a theses or dissertation: Touch it every day.

This chapter describes the elements of a master's-level thesis and doctoral dissertation involving primary research.

TIPS SPECIFICALLY RELATED TO THE ORIGINAL RESEARCH PROCESS

The following are some tips specifically related to theses and dissertations:

1. Start with a question that is of interest or relevance. Because you will be living with this question for a while, make sure it is of interest and it is connected somehow to your professional or personal life.
2. After you have your initial question, begin your review of the literature. Theoretical articles will provide important theoretical context for your study; however, because you are conducting research, reviewing research studies related to your question will be especially important. These studies can be used to inform your own study. Review them to see what questions have been asked, how they have been asked, and how they have been answered. Here, you will find valuable insights to inform the methodology used in your own study. Remember: New knowledge builds on existing knowledge.
3. Design your proposal based on your review of the literature (see Chapter 26). You do not need to include all the research studies reviewed for your proposal (although more is always better), but your sample should be an objective representative of the field. Avoid subjectivity by omission and inclusion.

4. Remember that you are not proving anything. This is stated in Chapter 22 but is worth repeating. Your research will gather data used to (a) support or not support a hypothesis, (b) answer a research question, (c) provide evidence in support of something, or (d) understand a phenomenon, condition, experience, or situation. There will be results or findings, followed by conclusions, implications, or applications of your results, but you are not proving anything.

5. If your study involves human subjects (as do most studies with the social sciences), then you will need to fill out Institutional Review Board (IRB) forms and requirements. The IRB review is designed to ensure that the appropriate steps are taken to protect the rights and welfare of subjects or participants involved in research. IRB names and processes may vary slightly at each institution.

Research is the process of asking questions and using data to answer these questions (Johnson, 2012). Original research uses one of the methods of science described in Chapter 22 to generate data. Theses and dissertations involving original research have five chapters. Each element is described here.

CHAPTER I: INTRODUCTION

Start with the introduction to the topic (no heading for this section). Identify the problem, and state any general questions related to the area of inquiry. Also, provide a sense of why this inquiry is important.

Background Information

Use a centered heading. The title of this heading should be related to the background information you are providing. Although you may have as many as three sections here, it is important to keep this chapter as short as possible. Provide only enough information to help the reader understand the problem or question and put the purpose of your study in a meaningful context.

Purpose of the Study

Use a centered heading. In one sentence, describe the purpose of the study. Then, describe the subjects or participants and treatment or conditions:

- **An example for a quantitative study:** The purpose of this study was to investigate the effects of thinking-skills instruction on students' writing. The sample consisted of 167 elementary students assigned to one of two groups: an experimental group in which classroom teaching implemented thinking-skills lessons and a comparison group that received no treatment. This study explores whether thinking-skills instruction improved students' ability to generate and organize their ideas for writing.

- **An example for a qualitative study:** The purpose of this study was to investigate middle school students' use of humor. The researcher spent 6 months in a suburban middle school near Minneapolis that had 356 students in Grades 6 through 8. Data were collected using field notes, student interviews and surveys, and teacher interviews. The researcher wanted to explore students' use of humor in negotiating their social, emotional, and academic worlds.

Figure 28.1   Chapter I

CHAPTER I
INTRODUCTION

Background Information

Purpose of the Study

CHAPTER II: REVIEW OF THE LITERATURE

This review of the literature begins the same as in secondary research. Use academic books and journal articles to build theoretical context and describe research studies that can support or inform your question, hypothesis, or problem statement. It ends with the research questions.

Statement of Specific Research Questions

Use a centered heading. This section states your research questions and, for quantitative studies, describes the measures used to answer them. These are at the heart of the study, as everything that follows is designed to answer these questions. Be concise yet specific here:

- An example for a quantitative study: This study will seek to answers four questions:

1. Will thinking-skills instruction demonstrate a significant effect on students' ability to generate ideas for writing? This will be measured by comparing scores and change scores on students' prewriting samples.

2. Will thinking-skills instruction demonstrate a significant effect on students' ability to organize their ideas for writing? This will be measured by comparing scores

and change scores on the Jones Holistic Writing Assessment (Jones Assessment Company, 2002). Student and teacher surveys and interviews will also be used here.

3. Do students perceive thinking-skills instruction to be useful? This will be measured using a Likert-type rating scale to assess students' attitudes and perceptions. Student and teacher surveys and interviews will also be used here.

4. Do teachers perceive thinking skills instruction to be effective? This will be measured using a Likert-type rating scale to assess students' attitudes and perceptions. Student and teacher surveys and interviews will also be used here.

- An example for a qualitative study: This qualitative research will seek to investigate three areas:

1. What kind of humor do students use? What are the humor-related topics? Who are the subjects of the humor?

2. In what situations do students use humor? How do the delivery and content of humor change from varying situations?

3. What are the social, emotional, and academic contexts of humor? Is there an aggressive element in humor? Are there varying purposes for the use of humor?

Figure 28.2   Chapter II

CHAPTER II
REVIEW OF THE LITERATURE

Statement of Specific Research Questions

CHAPTER III: METHODOLOGY

This chapter describes the subjects, materials, procedures, and the design and analyses used in your study. Past tense is used to describe all aspects of methodology.

Subjects, Sources, or Participants

Use a centered heading. The title of this varies according to the type of study. Quantitative and qualitative studies are described differently. Describe the humans or materials. If humans are used, then the reader should know the age, where they came from, how they were chosen, number, and gender breakdown. If humans are not used, describe what is being examined. Also included here is a description of the setting, conditions, or environment in which the study takes place.

Materials

Use a centered heading. Describe any materials used in the study. This may include materials used in the treatment as well as any measuring or data collection devices, such as rating scales, rubrics, field notes, or survey instruments.

Procedures

Use a centered heading. Describe how the study was organized and conducted and how data were collected. This should be a recipe for your study written in such a way that another person could read and replicate it. Describe the treatment (for quantitative studies) and how you went about collecting data.

Design and Analysis

Use a centered heading. For quantitative studies, identify the independent variables and the dependent variables. For qualitative studies, describe the conditions. For both, describe the experimental design, and tell how the data were analyzed.

Figure 28.3   Chapter III

CHAPTER III
METHODOLOGY

Subjects, Sources, or Participants

Materials

Procedures

Design and Analysis

CHAPTER IV: RESULTS

This chapter presents the results of the study. Because research happens in a specific instant in time, use past tense to describe all results. Listed here are just the data or facts. Conclusions or inferences related to these are usually saved for the last chapter. Use tables and figures as necessary. Create a centered heading for each question, and describe the results below them:

- An example for a quantitative study: Will students receiving thinking-skills instruction demonstrate a significant change in their abilities to generate ideas? This was measured by comparing scores and change scores on students' prewriting samples. The data were analyzed using a 2×2 analysis of variance with the variables being the two treatment groups. The analysis of variance for the writing scores is shown in Table 4.1.
- An example for a qualitative study: What kind of humor do students use, and what are the topics and subjects of this humor? The type of humor most often used by these middle school students was the sexual reference and word play. Table 4.1 shows the types of humor and the frequency of their use. Table 4.1 also shows the difference in gender, with males using more sexual humor while females used more personal attack humor.

CHAPTER V: DISCUSSION

This chapter contains an overview of the study, a summary of results, conclusions, limitations of the study, and recommendations or practical implications.

Overview of the Study

Use a centered heading. Restate the purpose of the study, and briefly describe how the results were obtained.

Summary of Results

Use a centered heading. Provide a brief summary of the results. Present these results in the same order as they appeared in Chapter IV.

Conclusions

Use a centered heading. Move beyond the data to tell what the results mean, and describe possible implications. Using subheadings, organize the conclusions around each research question.

Limitations of the Study

Use a centered heading. Describe the research goal and any limitations of the study. That is, what data might have been missed by the design? Based on this, describe limitations for the application of the results.

Recommendations

Use a centered heading. Describe how the results might be used or applied, and provide ideas for future research.

Figure 28.4   Chapter V

CHAPTER V
DISCUSSION

Overview of the Study

Summary of Results

Conclusions

Limitations of the Study

Recommendations

REFERENCES AND APPENDIXES

References and appendixes for original research are presented in the same way as with secondary research.

THE LAST WORD

This chapter ends with three tips for completing your thesis or dissertation: First, pace yourself. The thesis and dissertation is a marathon, not a sprint. Think in terms of months, not weeks. Second, set goals and deadlines for each component of your project, and focus only on that component. This will keep you from becoming overwhelmed. And finally, touch it every day. Even if you spend 5 minutes rereading a couple of paragraphs, it is important to touch your project every day. This helps to keep your unconscious mind actively engaged even when your conscious mind is focusing on other things.

Conclusion

The Last Word, Not the Final Word

This book is not meant to be the final word on any of the topics described. Nothing is the final word on anything. However, it should provide a foundation and framework for you to understand the various components of academic and professional writing. As mentioned in the introduction of this book, good writers learn their craft and develop their writing abilities over time. It is not difficult if you understand the process. However, it does take practice, experience, reflection, and a desire to improve.

About the Author

Andrew Johnson is a graduate of Grantsburg High School in Grantsburg, Wisconsin. He attended the University of Wisconsin–River Falls, where he graduated with a B.S. degree in Music and Speech-Communication. After earning elementary teaching licensure, he taught 2nd grade in River Falls, Wisconsin from 1983 to 1986. He went on to teach in elementary schools in the Twin Cities area and also spent three years working in the Grantsburg School District as a 5th grade teacher and the gifted education coordinator.

He earned his Ph.D. from the University of Minnesota in Literacy Education in 1997. He is works at Minnesota State University, Mankato as a professor of literacy in the Department of Special Education, where he specializes in literacy instruction for students with reading difficulties. He is the author of 10 books and numerous academic articles related to literacy, learning, teacher development, and the human condition.

He lives in North Mankato with his wife, Dr. Nancy Fitzsimons, and his dogs, Mickey and Emmet.